YOU WERE DESTINED TO BE TOGETHER

A Zen Approach to Soul Mates

by
Tom Arbino

PO Box 754, Huntsville, AR 72740
800-935-0045 or 479-738-2348 fax 479-738-2448
www.ozarkmt.com

For permission, serialization, condensation, adaptions, or for our catalog of other publications, write to Ozark Mountain Publishing, Inc., P.O. box 754, Huntsville, AR 72740, ATTN: Permissions Department.

Library of Congress Cataloging-in-Publication Data
Arbino, Tom, 1958-
   You Were Destined to be Together, by Tom Arbino
A Zen approach to attracting your soulmate.

1. Soulmates   2. Zen Approach   3. Relationships 4. Metaphysics
I. Arbino, Tom, 1958-   II. Soulmates   III. Metaphysics
IV. Title

Library of Congress Catalog Card Number: 2010939623

ISBN: 978-1-886940-734

Cover Art and Layout: www.enki3d.com
Book set in: Times New Roman
Book Design: Julia Degan

Published by:

**OZARK
MOUNTAIN
PUBLISHING**

PO Box 754
Huntsville, AR 72740

WWW.OZARKMT.COM
Printed in the United States of America

Table of Contents

INTRODUCTION

There is a higher and faster way to attract your soul mate, and that way is Zen. While using the Zen meditations that I am going to show you, the distance between you and your soul mate will vanish, instantly bringing the two of you together. Unlocking the deeper mind and your past life connections to your soul mate are the keys to reuniting with your soul mate in this life.

Trying to find someone who is suited to you on-line or in the personals is like trying to find a shiny 1983D penny in all the pennies in the US Mint. Unless you employ your unconscious mind and the deeper (spiritual) aspects of being with your soul mate, the chances of you finding this person are minimal. Many people end up marrying the wrong person, never finding their soul mate in this incarnation and having a relationship that is much less than the relationship that they are supposed to have.

Many people confuse religious beliefs with a soul mate, believing that the two of them were meant to serve the dogma of a particular church. This will rarely meet the karmic conditions that serve as the foundation of the soul mate relationship. This relationship is more than mere dogma since the karma of the soul mate relationship encompasses the karma of the children that you will have as well. I will explain this in detail in the *Your family was destined* chapter.

Whether you know it or not, a good portion of you coming together with your soul mate is to have the children that you are destined to have. You aren't being drawn together for selfish or dogmatic reasons, but rather for larger, karmic reasons that span several life times. Your children were most likely key players in your past lives, reincarnating with you again to balance old karma and to give all of you an opportunity to grow spiritually.

Contrary to what many people would have you believe, you can't draw your soul mate to you whenever you please. The time must be right. There are lessons that you need to learn first and if you haven't learned these lessons and advanced beyond them, then finding your soul mate will be of little use to you. Keep in mind, that your soul mate and the karmic lessons involved are one in the same.

If a man who is meant to be an equal partner with his soul mate is still womanizing, then his soul mate will take wings and fly away fast. He must overcome his womanizing and see women in a higher way. This is the karmic lesson that he needs to learn *before* he meets his soul mate, and the time won't be right for him to meet his soul mate until he does so. To try and draw this person to him before he has learned this lesson would be like trying to punch his way through a brick wall.

Zen can make up for the shortfalls that other soul mate techniques leave out. Most soul mate books use simple meditations, chants, and Tarot cards that do little to draw your soul mate to you. The advanced Zen meditations that I am going to teach you use the crown charka, which will connect you to the spirit world, and constitutes that highest spiritual meditation known to man. The Zen that I am going to teach you isn't Zazen based Zen, but a new, American Zen called Crown Chakra Zen.

Here is the meditation you should use to see what karmic lessons you need to learn before you meet your soul mate. Knowing just what these lessons are will keep you from guessing, steering you in the right direction that will lead you to meeting your soul mate, and allowing you to cast off the delusions and nonsense that have been preventing you from meeting your soul mate. Get into a meditative state. See a sphere of pure white light at your crown charka. Take a few moments to see this sphere pulsate. Now see yourself riding a bicycle down a country road while continuing to see the sphere of pure white light at your crown chakra pulsate. You will come upon the karmic lessons that you need to learn. Don't stop at the first one, but journey down the road a ways.

It would be helpful to know the exact date that you will meet your soul mate and the exact date of your wedding, if any.

Knowing these dates doesn't mean that you can merely kick back and do nothing. Knowing these dates—along with the karmic lessons that you need to learn—will chart the course that you need to go in. This is much different than calling your soul mate to you, which isn't going work unless you learn the karmic lessons that you need to learn.

Here is the meditation that you need to do. Get into a meditative state and see a sphere of pure white light at your crown charka. Take a few moments to see it pulsate. Now see yourself reading a newspaper. State that you want to know the exact date that you will meet your soul mate. Flip through the pages of the newspaper. As you are turning these pages, you will see a date. You can do the same thing for the date of your wedding while still in the same meditation. Start with the front page, see your crown chakra pulsate and state that you want to see the date of your wedding. Flip through the pages. If you get to the end and still don't see a date, that means that you won't marry your soul mate. Keep in mind that these dates are correct *at the moment* that you see them. Circumstances change and so might the date.

When seeking your soul mate, it is best to advance spiritually since you are on a spiritual journey. The best way to go about this is to develop your crown charka. The meditation that I am about to show you will lead to enlightenment if you practice it religiously. This is the central meditation of Crown Chakra Zen, which will connect you to the spirit world and make God within your unconscious, what Jung called the Self, conscious. Developing your crown charka is the most spiritually advanced thing that you can do. Buddha's crown chakra looked like it was on fire, and if you can develop your crown chakra only a small percentage of that, then you will be one of the most spiritually advanced people on the planet.

Here is the meditation that you need to do. You should do this meditation everyday, twice a day if possible. First, get into a meditative state. Now see an eye at your third eye charka, in the center of your forehead. See the eyelid closed, seeing it open slowly to reveal an eye with a pupil the color of your choice. See red capillaries in the white portion. When the eyelid is all the way open, see a line of white light going from the eye to your crown chakra. Once it is there, see the crown chakra pulsate with white light. Let the line and eye vanish and focus only on your crown chakra. See a sphere of pure white light at your crown chakra. It might help you to visualize the light inside a light bulb. Chant *shine,* and every time that you do, see the sphere at your crown chakra pulsate with white light. Do this for at least five minutes.

The quest to finding your soul mate need not be a long one, one of struggling, or one that involves pain. The question is all in how you *choose* to view it. Your quest will involve learning, and that learning can either speed you up or slow you down, the choice is yours. It is best not to resist but to go where your quest for true love takes you. If you resist, you will only find pain and push your soul mate further away from you. But if you don't resist and go willingly where you need to go, then your soul mate will come running to you.

THE NATURE OF LOVE

L ove is saying that I am here for you. To love someone is to want them near you, to want to nurture them and support their every need. Love is the gentle hand that caresses. This is the love that everyone desires. This is the love that comes from a soul mate.

It is essential to understand the nature of love before a soul mate can be sought and the Zen meditations that I am going to teach you will cascade you into higher levels. Love is a commodity in our society, one that is packaged and sold on TV. Most of us have a false notion of what love is. American love is conditional love, and it rarely goes beyond the surface. This sort of love is all about the ego and its cravings. This is clearly seen in the man who chooses the "trophy wife," basing his decision only upon looks and breast size. Women will choose a man with a good corporate job even if they aren't compatible. These issues soon give way to the roles they fall into. Ego love is doomed to fail.

Conditional love is centered on *things*. A woman marries a lawyer because a lawyer is a brand name that is assigned a good salary and a position in society. The lawyer marries the woman because she's attractive and it's expected of him. A woman might date a cute beachcomber or even have an affair with him, but when it comes to marriage, the husband's occupation has just as much to do with the decision as does how handsome he is. An average looking attorney is "husband material" by his brand name alone.

This sort of love always judges—I love you if you're a college graduate and make $40,000 a year, I love you if you give me sex, or I love you if.... The entire relationship becomes a series of trade offs and if one end were to fall through, such as the husband losing his job, then the love is withdrawn (unless the husband gets another job fast). Though not everyone is this shallow, it has been heard of a man divorcing his wife because she gets breast cancer. She is no longer a *role* or a *thing*.

College is the stomping ground where future corporate brides and grooms size each other up. Most women will choose a guy that they think is going somewhere, with a house in the suburbs, two cars, etc being the objective. Dating is a game with a well-worn path to the corporate suite. Fraternities and sororities serve as brand names, and not everyone is considered equal. Words such as "pre-law" or "business administration" become labels that men wear, and everyone knows who wears what label. Those who aren't Greek are confined to be in a lower league, but the labels exist just the same.

Roles are commodities in America, with the actual person in the role irrelevant. TV shows parade men around like Ken dolls, but they aren't Dick, Bob, or Chuck. They're attorneys, executives, and blue-collar guys. The TV shows reveal every detail of what goes along with a doctor or lawyer. The woman can see where she's going to live, what kind of furniture she's going to have, the car she'll drive, etc.

In our society, only certain people are deemed loveable. A guy in a wheel chair is deemed to be someone who doesn't want love, someone who is content to spend the rest of his life playing wheel chair basketball and not even interested in members of the opposite sex. Such a person isn't deemed worthy of the "reward" of a girlfriend, and people talk to him accordingly. If he were to say that he was dating, they would be shocked. If they were to discover that his girlfriend could walk and "wasn't like him" they would be beyond shocked.

The saddest thing of all is that many people in this world aren't loved. They are raised by parents who have no business having children, many of them being so abused that even the greatest love cannot reverse the damage that has been done. Such people live a life that is less than human.

To deny someone love, especially during the formative years, is to condemn them to a psychological death. Such people are emotionally immature and have many gaps in their lives. Most of them never marry, and of the ones that do, they are lacking in many other areas of their lives. Many people try to fill this gap with drugs, booze, money, sex, etc, but none of them fill the void that was left by love. This will only lead to addictions and obsessions, which will have to be leaned on more the longer there is no love to fill the void.

They seek love in other ways, substituting other things for love. These people often become workaholics. They seek respect and admiration from their boss, working hard to please him. They become hard, repressing their emotions, denying love its very existence. Many of these people go far in the corporate world but sadly, this is all that they have. They don't know how to relate to anyone outside of work, which has consumed their entire social life.

This can take on twisted and hard aspects and in extreme cases, even lead to murder or suicide. Many of these extreme cases turn up in doctors' offices, showing up time and time again. Medical attention becomes a substitute for love, and many of these people carve so much attention that it distracts the doctor from other patients. These people will call almost everyday, set up one appointment after another, and still be in pain after batteries of tests.

In extreme cases, this pathological need for attention is transferred to the children of these people. Medicine even has a name for this disease, Munchausen by proxy. The person will actually make their own child sick—by giving it pills, poison, laxatives, etc—and then rush the child to the doctor and insist that all kinds of tests be run. What a far better world we would live in if parents would unconditionally love their children.

If you want love, shallow and conditional love, then you must be loveable. By loveable I mean what society considers worthy of love. Billions are spent on trying to make us loveable.

Anything from hair products, crash diets, the latest clothes, etc are sought after. The whole youth dating scene is a sizing up grounds, with partners not loving the person as they are, but sizing them up as potential marriage partners. One of the ways in which they size them up is to fantasize about what it would be like to be the spouse of their date. No fantasy, no second date.

Most young people go into the dating scene without knowing what they want in a partner. They go from date to date, trying on each one for size. Most people end up getting married the same way, without ever truly deciding what they want. They will marry for approval, religious reasons, status, security, etc, but rarely for spiritual reasons. Most of these people don't even realize that they have a soul mate, let alone seek out their soul mate or find their soul mate.

Here is a better way to realize that you are loved even if no one in this world loves you. Get into a meditative state and see a sphere of pure white light at your heart, seeing it rise several inches above your heart. See this sphere both rise and pulsate with white light and every time you do, chant *shine*. Do this everyday for at least five minutes. You may feel some tightness in your chest. This won't harm you, it is only your heart charka loosening.

Shannon J. came to me after a relationship that she had been in for two years came to an end.

She asked me, "How do I know when someone is husband material?"

I told her, "There's no such thing as husband material."

"But there are certain qualities that make a man an ideal husband," she insisted.

"You only think that there are, but no such qualities exist. Any man is capable of being a good husband," I said.

"But this magazine had this quiz in it with all these qualities that psychologists say make an ideal husband," she said.

"They sell a lot of magazines with stuff like that, but what it really boils down to is entertainment. It's just another magazine article, one having little scientific value," I told her.

"So how do I find a good man?" she asked.

"You have to decide what you want. I don't mean a good looking guy with a great job, but what you really want in a man," I said.

"What do you mean?" She asked.

"Do you want someone to be there for you emotionally?" I asked her.

"Of course I do," she replied.

"Do you want someone to listen to you?" I inquired.

"Doesn't everybody? What are you driving at?" She looked at me with a puzzled look on her face.

"This is what you have to seek in a man, not money and a position in society," I told her.

"So I should forget about money and position?"

"Yes, these things are only names and forms. You need to see your soul mate in a higher way."

"What do you mean, 'a higher way'?" She looked at me with a perplexed look on her face.

"You need to see his true nature. Not the body or things that he can buy, but the true him."

"What do you mean?" She asked.

"See his spirit, his personality, and not the outward things that surround him."

"A good personality is nice, but I want to have children and have a house in the suburbs. This is what I visualized ever since I was a little girl."

"Most people want the same things and it is merely a delusion," I replied.

"How can a house in the suburbs be a delusion?" She wondered.

"It is a delusion because it isn't the true nature of love. You are confusing symbols with love itself. You need to go

5

deeper. The true nature of love doesn't have to do with things. You are trying to find it out there, but there is no love out there, only objects that we have been told are love."

"But we have to live somewhere."

"You have relegated your soul mate to a thing, an object, and a possession. You have equated what is eternal with what is temporary."

"I still don't understand."

"Do you think that house in the suburbs was there when you and your soul mate were together in your past life? How about the incarnation before that?"

She gazed down at her feet for a moment, and then said, "I don't think so."

"Seek what is eternal, not what is temporary and what will decay. The love of your soul mate transcends many centuries, spanning many life times. By focusing on what is subject to decay and nonexistence, you are clinging to delusions that you think are eternal."

"This is what everyone has been taught."

"Yes, society teaches you things that are false because they don't want you to discover the truth. Society wants you to conform to what they tell you and to believe as they tell you to believe."

She looked at me with a puzzled look on her face for a moment or so. She then asked, "So I shouldn't be like everybody else?"

"Right. The things that society wants you to focus on are only temporary and things that are based upon the ego. These are the things that will lead you to the wrong man and lead you to a man that is associated with these temporary things."

"So how will I know the difference? How will I know my soul mate?" She asked with wide eyes.

"When you first meet your soul mate, you will have a funny feeling that you knew him in the past. This is because you are unconsciously recognizing the same soul that you were with in a past life."

Here is the meditation that will bring your soul mate to you. This meditation uses the advanced techniques of Crown Chakra Zen, and is the most powerful soul mate technique ever developed. Other soul mate techniques only use meditation. By using the crown chakra, you will call your soul mate to you from the span of many lifetimes.

You have to decide exactly what you want if you plan to attract your soul mate. Take out a sheet of paper and carefully write down the qualities that you want in your soul mate. This may take you several days or even several weeks. Forget the shallow things such as looks, money, position in society, etc. Focus on what you really want—someone to listen to you, someone to hold you, someone who is spiritual, someone with common interests, etc.

When you have finished with the list, and be sure to put some time and thought into it, you need to be sure that you are alone and won't be disturbed by anyone. Get into a meditative state. See a sphere of pure white light at your crown charka. Take a few moments to see it pulsate with white light.

Now take the list and read the first quality on your soul mate list. See the words of that quality come off the page as text and go into the sphere at your crown charka. See the sphere pulse with white light. Now do the same with the next quality, proceeding with care and paying attention to your visualization. Keep going until you have finished the list. Now close your eyes and chant *shine,* and every time you do so, see the sphere pulsate with white light. Do this for at least five minutes once a day, twice a day if possible. This meditation will draw your soul mate to you like a magnet.

In addition to this meditation, you have to change your thinking. What you think at every moment of the day shapes your reality. If you want a soul mate, then you can't shut that person

7

out in your thinking. Think only positive and loving thoughts. I know this sounds easy, but it's really a tall order. Only Christ or Buddha could do it every moment, and this is why they became overflowing fountains of love.

The way to begin this is to stop yourself whenever you think a negative thought and replace it with a positive and loving thought. How often do you see someone or think of someone and judge them in your thinking? *Stop yourself the moment you do this.* Judge no one. Criticize no one. What goes on in your head is what goes on outside of you. If you think loving thoughts, people will be more loving toward you.

Reflect on the qualities of your soul mate often. Smile and think of them positively, experience the joy of being in love. The more you charge them with positive emotions, the stronger they will become. Think about them in this way just before falling off to sleep at night, and tell your higher self to bring this person to you. In this way, you will also put your unconscious mind to work for you in drawing your soul mate to you.

By changing what is in your deeper mind, you will change your reality. Replace thoughts of being alone, unloved, not going out on a date on Saturday night, etc with loving thoughts. The way that you go about this is to stop thinking about being alone the moment that the thought arises. It's important that you don't visualize a specific person. When the thought or image of being alone comes to mind, replace it with the joy of being in love. Visualize the joy of being in love, experiencing it to the point of it being real.

Unconditional love is not a myth; but rather it is an experience that can be lived. You must accept this. If you want to experience unconditional love, then you must stop judging others and accept them just the way they are. Come to realize that you can't change another person, so give up your need to control him/her. Quit expecting him/her to be what you want him/her to be.

This often meets an impasse when a girl brings a boy home to meet her parents, specifically the father. The parents, instead of accepting him as he is, want to change him. They have an image in their minds of what kind of boy is right for their daughter, and no one could ever live up to that image. Parents can kill unconditional love. They have too many conditions that they want to place on it. You have to get around this.

You don't have to be defensive or aggressive, but you have to stand behind your decision to love unconditionally. Others will test you, insist that you explain yourself or do as so and so is doing, but you can't let it get inside your head and change your thinking. You must be a beacon of unconditional love among this sea of negativity. You will be poked and prodded to conform. To be just like everybody else, etc, but you must step aside and let these things pass without giving them so much as a single thought. And then you will rise above the masses.

Becky P. had been married for over ten years when she began having problems in her relationship.

She came to me and said, "I always thought Curt was my soul mate, but now I don't know any more. I try to love him unconditionally, but it keeps getting harder and harder."

"What's going on?" I asked her.

"He has this annoying habit of running around the house in his underwear. He sits and watches TV wearing nothing but his briefs. He even does it while we have company over," she said.

"You're trying to change him and this is what is causing you grief," I said.

"But he never did this before. We were married for nine years and he never did it in all that time. It keeps getting worse and worse," she said.

"You have to accept him the way he is without trying to change him," I said.

"But I have to change him. It's become an embarrassment. People are starting to talk," she said.

"What happened at the time that that he started running around the house in his underwear?" I asked.

"I don't know." She looked at me with a puzzled look on her face.

"So what happened as he did it more and more?" I probed.

"We stopped bowling on Wednesday nights, but that couldn't be it," she said.

"Does he get dressed for work?" I asked.

"Yeah, and that's what I don't understand. He never used to care about that old factory uniform that he puts on, but he's asking me to sew even small holes and to get stains out that he's never cared about before," she said.

"So when was the last time you had any romance or adventure?" I asked.

Becky's head dropped, and she stared at her shoes for some time before responding, "It's been awhile. But we're so busy with the kids and–"

I interrupted, "You're in a deep rut. You need some adventure in your life, everybody does. Curt doesn't have anything to get excited about, so he doesn't care what he wears around the house or what other people think."

"So what should I do?" She asked with wide eyes.

"Add some excitement to the house. Surprise him when he comes home from work. Have candles burning, make him a special meal, and wear a see-through negligee."

"I'll try it." She smiled.

"Your focus is centered on the kids—" I began.

"That's so true," she interrupted, her face lighting up.

"You need to be a couple again and do the things you did while you were dating."

Her face lit up even more while she replied, "That is so true."

"Even soul mates can become stagnant and just because you're married to your soul mate that doesn't mean you can put your relationship on auto pilot and stop working at it."

"You are so right!" Her face lit up.

"Your love must continue to grow and branch out into new things even if you have kids."

"We haven't done anything new in years. All we do is take care of the kids."

"Most of your relationship is probably centered on money."

"We just never seem to have enough of it."

"There's more to a marriage than just paying bills. Don't make it the only thing that your marriage is about or even a major focus of your marriage. Make the major focus of your marriage romance and adventure."

L ove needs adventure or it simply isn't love any more. People call it all sorts of things—*I love him, but I'm no longer "in love" with him,* or they claim to have "fallen out" of love. Many people in this situation have an affair, believing that the excitement of an affair will add some excitement to their stagnant relationship. This never works and if the other partner is paying attention, they will wonder what their partner is so excited about (a telltale sign of an affair).

The affair provides the excitement that the partner craves. The whole routine of wondering if you will get caught, secret phone calls and rendezvouses all fuel the excitement even more. The tired cliché is true, if he doesn't want it at home he's getting it somewhere else. The reverse is also true, if he's getting it at home he's not going to look for it anywhere else.

There's nothing magical about having a soul mate. You still have to work at the relationship, and you still have to keep it exciting and new. This will become harder and harder as the relationship progresses, but this is the reality of love.

Love renewal technique

This time I want you to make two lists, or you can just draw a line down the middle of a sheet of paper. At the top of the left-hand column write the word *stagnant*. On the right side write the word *excitement*. Take as long as you need, it may take several hours or several days. It might be better to go through it and then let it sit for a day or two and go over it again.

Write down the things that you feel are stagnant in your relationship, and try to be as honest as possible. These usually include some pretty mundane things—sitting around watching TV, taking the kids to soccer, etc. Now consider the things that are, *or have,* excited you about your relationship. These usually include some things that have probably fallen by the wayside—he used to chase me around the kitchen and then make love to me, he called me from work to whisper sweet nothings in my ear, etc.

Once you have each list together, and you can either do this as a couple or individually, I want you to wait until the apartment is quiet and you're all alone. If both partners are doing this, each person should do this next part by him/herself without the other partner present.

Do the *soul mate meditation* as described earlier in this chapter. Get into a meditative state and then see a sphere of pure white light at your crown chakra. Read the *stagnant* list and see each one go into the sphere as text. When you have finished, chant *shine* and see the sphere pulsate with white light every time you do.

Now take the *excitement* list. Read over each item, pausing after you have read each one. See each item going into the sphere as text after you have read it. When you have finished, I want you to put the list down and meditate in the same way.

THE NATURE OF SOUL MATES

A soul mate is the other half of us, the one that we need to become whole. Plato went as far as to say that the soul is split into two halves and that we spend our entire life searching for the other half. This isn't correct, each soul is an individual. Plato demonstrated the strength of our longing for that other half that makes us whole. This other soul is there to teach us karmic lessons that we need for growth. A soul mate will help us to balance the karma that we need to balance in order to advance spiritually.

A friend of mine named Karla is a meek woman. She thought that her soul mate would be a big, strong man who would take care of her, and take the lead in the relationship. To her surprise, her soul mate was just as meek as she was. Not long after they were married, he broke his leg and had to have surgery. He had to have several pins put in and Karla soon had to be the bread winner in order to make ends meet.

Karla thought her soul mate relationship would be much different than it was. She underwent past life regression and quickly found that she was a woman on the prairie and her husband was a big, burly man. She completely depended upon him for food, water, wood to cook with, etc. One day he went hunting and never returned. Instead of going out to get food etc, she sat there and waited for him. She starved to death.

Karla's taking charge in her current marriage was just the karmic lesson that she needed to learn in order to advance spiritually. It wasn't long after she became comfortable in the lead role in the relationship that her husband made a remarkable recovery. She never fully relinquished control of the relationship back to him, keeping her job and even putting a few bucks aside for emergencies.

A soul mate is someone you were involved with many times before—the relationship spanning several lifetimes. The person that you are seeking, who is also seeking you, has helped you many times before. The purpose of a soul mate is to help you lose your worldly delusions and to advance to the higher levels of consciousness. Though you can do this without a soul mate, it is usually only Zen monks or others who are spiritually advanced enough to make it that far alone.

A soul mate is a catalyst to your unfolding, boosting you further along the path than anyone else can. You can only go so far on your own. Only a hermit or Buddha can unfold all the way to enlightenment alone in a cave. The rest of us need others to help and support us. Though a group can be helpful, a soul mate will propel you much farther than you could even conceive of going in your wildest dreams.

A soul mate is someone that has a shared purpose with you. Some soul mates are for life, though others come into your life only to complete a task or help you from one stage to the other. A soul mate is rarely only about love or sex, unless you have some reason for this. A soul mate encompasses every aspect of you, causing you to unfold on levels that you didn't know you had in you.

Someone doesn't become a soul mate overnight; in fact it takes several lifetimes. The two souls will grow and unfold to levels far greater than one can achieve in a single lifetime. Each time the souls learn another lesson, it is hoped, they create new karma. You have more than one soul mate, but you may only meet one during this incarnation. You may not need the other soul mate for karmic reasons and thus this person may not even incarnate in your current life.

You can search your past lives for any soul mates that you had in the past or to check and see if the person you are with now is someone you were with in a past life. Chances are if a person is helping you now that same person has helped you in the past. The people in your life play different roles in each incarnation and it is important that you know what these roles are. In order to fully understand these roles, you need to undergo past life regression.

Here is a meditation that will allow you to search your past lives. The first thing you have to do is make sure you're alone and that you won't be interrupted. Make the house quiet. You can light a candle or some incense if you feel so inclined. You have to both protect yourself and attune your body to the astral plane. The first step in doing this is to balance your chakras.

Visualize a bright, white sphere about a foot above your head. See the sphere shining brighter and brighter. See a white shaft of light coming down from the sphere and touching your crown chakra. See a bright white sphere rising from your crown chakra. See that sphere spinning and see anything that is impure is being cast away. See that light becoming whiter.

Now, see a shaft of white light coming down from your crown chakra and going to your third eye chakra. See a bright white sphere coming out of it. Repeat the above balancing and cleansing ritual and then see a shaft of white light going to your throat chakra. Keep going until you have done all seven of your chakras.

Now, see spheres of white light spinning and glowing brightly at each of your chakras. See the bright white sphere at your heart chakra expanding to cocoon your entire body in a white sphere. Hold this image for a moment and then let it fade.

Sit still, a meditative position works best. Breathe in a 2/4 rhythm—inhale for a count of 2, hold your breath for a moment, and then exhale for a count of 4. Keep going until you bring upon a meditative state.

Close your eyes. State in your private speech what past life you want to explore:

I want to see if I was with Susan in a past life. I instruct my higher self to go to the past life that I need to explore now.

It is best if you visualize the person, as they are now,

15

when you say this. Hold onto this image for a moment or so. You may want to make a tape of what follows.

See yourself going to a door. You open that door and step through it. Inside is a spiral staircase that only goes down, going farther down than you can see. You walk down, going around and around, traveling even further down. Keep going down, going round and round the spiral staircase.

You come to a landing, and before you is a long corridor. At the end of the corridor is a white light—a light that is your past life. There is a barrel at the bottom of the steps. Get in it and roll toward the end of the corridor, knowing that as soon as you step out of the barrel at the end of the corridor you will be in your past life. Tell yourself that you are going to see vivid images of your past life as you are in the barrel. You get closer to the end of the corridor and then closer still. The barrel rolls out the end and into the white light. You get out of it.

You should be seeing vivid images of your past life. If you aren't, ask yourself some questions. *Where am I? Who am I with? What am I wearing? Am I outside or inside? Is it winter or summer?*

If you're new to this, you may have to repeat this several times before you see anything. Know that all the information from your past lives is stored in your unconscious mind and that the veil can be lifted. Don't think of the images and information as being in the spirit world or in any way separate from you. Also, don't think that you are doing something that is forbidden or believe the guilt trip that the mainstream churches want to send you on.

When you are finished exploring your past life, breathe in a 2/4 rhythm. See yourself floating up, rising slowly as a balloon. Return to consciousness and open your eyes. You will remember the images or scene from the past life that you saw. You may not understand what you saw and may have to go back one or more times.

Most people have more than one soul mate in their lives. These soul mates are like tumblers on a combination lock; each designed to fall into place when the number comes up. It would be of little use to you if you met your soul mate before the time was right. Instead of balancing karma or learning what you need to learn, you may very well create bad karma.

This brings us to a central issue concerning soul mates, the issue of time. A soul mate won't come into your life until the time is right. You can push as hard as you want, but nothing is going to come. All the effort that you put into trying to get a soul mate will be futile. But when the time is right, and all those cosmic tumblers fall into place, you won't be able to get rid of your soul mate if you try. You may even desire time alone or have an important project at work that requires your time. Forget about it.

If you are only meant to be together for a specific period of time, then your soul mate will depart when the time is right. You can try whatever you want—you can cling, you can beg, you can try to be the perfect mate, but if he is meant to go, then let him go. Let him go in your thinking without judgment or blame. Wish him well and go on your way.

Robin J. had been living with her boyfriend for three years when an old problem began boiling over. Though she believed that Shawn was her soul mate and had uncovered two previous lives with him, there was always a wall between them. He never trusted her with the money, and she got a secret credit card that he didn't know about. When he found out about it, he exploded. He packed up a bunch of his things but stopped short of moving out. He took her credit cards and cut them into many pieces. She had to beg and plead with him just for grocery money, and at times their relationship barely hung together.

I hypnotized Robin and then brought her back to the life that was most affecting her.

"Where are you?" I asked her.

"I don't know. It looks like someplace from long ago," she said.

"Describe it," I instructed her.

"There's a big public square with what appears to be a bunch of people gathered. All the men have swords and are dressed like Romans, but I don't think it's Rome," she described.

"You deeper mind will reveal to you where you are. Ask it in your private speech," I instructed.

"It said Babylon," she said.

"What are you doing?" I asked.

"I'm walking around a market buying things. I'm trying to be careful because there are many cutthroats and thieves. A fight has broken out among some men in front of me. I have to stop," she said.

"Are you a man or a woman?" I asked.

"A woman," she said.

"And how old are you?" I asked.

"I'm still a maid. I'm only seventeen. My father is away and my mother is ill. I'm the oldest and I have to return with some food," she said.

"So you're spending money that your mother gave you?" I asked.

"Yes. It's all the money that our family has. If I lose it, we go hungry. My father is the only one who can hunt and he is away," she said.

"So what's happening? Are you spending your money wisely?" I asked.

"I bought a few apples, but I have to make my way to the meat. My mother is weak and needs some red meat to regain her strength," she said.

"So what's happening now?" I questioned.

"I'm still stopped. I'm watching the fight and-" Her voice became cut off.

"What's going on?" I asked.

"The fight is getting worse," she said.

"Is anyone trying to break it up?" I asked.

"No. There are no authority figures. I'm trying to move back, but there's a wall of people behind me," she said.

"Are they women trying to buy food?" I asked.

"No, most of them are men, who are cheering on the fight," she said.

"So what's going on now?" I asked.

"Uh-oh," she said.

"What happened?" I asked.

"I dropped my purse," she said.

"Were you clutching it? Did you drop it?" I asked.

"It was tied around my waist on a string. It came undone, or at least I think it did," she said.

"Do you have it?" I asked.

"No. Someone kicked it. I'm trying to find it on the ground but the crowd keeps ebbing and flowing around me. *There it is*," she said.

"Do you have it?" I asked.

"No, it's on the ground. I don't dare get down on all fours for fear of being trampled," she said.

"Does anybody else see it?" I asked.

"I don't...someone kicked it back toward me. I got it. I fixed it around my waist once again. In the commotion I lost the apples that I had bought," she said.

"Is the fight still going on?" I asked.

"Yes, but I'm trying to get out of it," she said.

"Now what do you see?" I probed.

"A man just got stabbed. The crowd moaned. I still can't make any progress. I abandoned all hopes of weaving my way through them and resigned myself to standing there until it's over," she said.

"What are the shop owners doing?" I asked.

"Most of them are...*oh no*," she said in a worried tone.

"What's happening?" I asked.

19

"Someone just snatched my purse with all my money in it. He's holding it by the string and twirling it around. He's saying, (She speaks in a deep and manly voice), "You stupid little girl. You walked all the way up here just to give me your money." Tears trickled out of each eye.

"So what's happening now?" I asked.

Her lips stammered, and she cried some more. She stared down at her feet.

"Tell me what's going on," I asked in a soft voice.

"It's him." Her voice broke.

"Who?" I asked.

"Shawn." She wiped her eyes. "He's the man who stole my purse."

I slowly brought her back to consciousness. When she opened her eyes, she burst into tears. She now understood why he didn't trust her with the money. Shawn believed that she would carelessly wear her purse on the outside of her gown instead of tucking it inside, especially in such a rough crowd.

Shawn underwent regression a few weeks later. I brought him to the lifetime that he shared with Robin.

"So what kind of guy were you? Look at yourself and tell me what you see?" I instructed him.

He paused for a prolonged moment, smacking his gums once or twice. His facial expression changed, and then he replied, "I'm a big brute of a guy. I stink, don't shave, and my teeth are yellow and rotten."

"Can you see yourself in the public square?" I questioned him.

"Yes," he said in a gasp.

"So what are you doing?"

"I'm the kind of guy who likes to push people around."

"Did you get involved in any fights?"

"Of course, that's what I'm there for."

"Did you win?"

He inhaled with a manly drawl, and then responded, "I fought one man and we were both evenly matched. We both walked away with bloody faces. I avowed revenge but deep inside I hoped that I never saw that man again."

"So then what happened?"

"I walked around for a while until I saw a guy who owed me some money."

"Was he a big guy like the last one?" I wondered.

"No." He paused for longer than a moment before continuing, "He was a little runt of a man."

"Describe what happened next," I instructed him.

"I felt a rage building inside of me. I decided to pound him, but I really wanted to stomp the man that I fought to a drawl."

"So what happened next?" I nudged him.

"I built the rage even higher, clinching my fists and then stormed up on the man. I shoved him up against the wall. He handed me his purse with a trembling hand. I knew that was all he had and I could've walked away, but I beat the man to a pulp. When I was finished, I withdrew my sword and bashed him in the mouth with the butt of the sword, knocking out a couple of teeth."

"Okay, I want you to move forward to the time when you snatched Robin's purse. Did you start the fight that erupted in the public square?" I asked.

"No, but it didn't take me long to join in."

"Did you punch anyone in particular?"

"I sought out small and weak men, ones that I could quickly get the upper hand with."

"So what happened?"

"Things didn't quite turn out the way that I expected. After taking a few stray blows in the head, I retreated."

"So how does Robin figure into all of this?"

"As I stood there breathing heavily, I saw her standing there. I saw her purse on her belt just hanging there and thought what a stupid little girl."

21

"So what happened next?" I prodded him.

"I sucked in my lips and decided to take her money. I ran up to her and snatched her purse. I gloated and twirled it around, taunting her about how stupid she was and how cleaver I was for taking her."

"And what did she do?"

His facial expression changed. He paused for longer than a moment, his gaze dropping. He inhaled with a wheeze, and then said, "She cried beyond control. She prayed and pleaded for God to help her. I thought it was just a few coins, but it meant much more to her than I thought. Her reaction surprised me."

"Did you think of giving the money back?"

"No, I repressed what I felt and continued to gloat. She ran away in tears. I told the man next to me what a pigeon I had plucked."

I led Shawn back into consciousness and he quickly realized how unfounded his fears were and got Robin replacement credit cards.

A soul mate will bring out what needs to grow in you. These areas will come to the surface so they can lead you to wholeness. The soul mate may have qualities that are either opposite or missing in you, qualities that you need to develop so that you can grow. Your soul mate will change you on every level, and that is what a soul mate is supposed to do.

Jung said that the union of opposites leads to wholeness and encounters with the God within—the Self. Unless you unite the other opposite, you will have areas in your life that are incomplete, areas that will become karma that you will need to resolve either later in this life or in a future incarnation. If you don't unite with your soul mate in this lifetime, then you will have to deal with it in your next life.

Higher self soul mate search

You can consult your higher self—God within your unconscious—about your soul mate or anything that you want. You need to make sure you won't be disturbed and that you are alone. You may want to light a candle and some incense, but this is optional.

Do the chakra balancing and white light protection as described above in the *past life soul mate search*. You need to do this every time you work with your higher self to insure that you are protected from any negativity.

Breathe in a 2/4 rhythm—inhaling for a count of 2, holding your breath for a moment, and exhaling for a count of 4. See a sphere about the size of a softball coming out of your crown chakra and hovering about a foot above your head. See it sparkling with pure white light.

Now you can ask it a question. It is best to only ask one question at a time and to keep it simple. Some questions you might want to ask are:

What do I need in my soul mate to lead me to wholeness?
Where will I meet my soul mate?
Am I ready for a soul mate at this time?
What is preventing me from having a soul mate?
What do I need to do in order to have a soul mate?

Once you have decided on the question, visualize the sphere and direct your attention to it. Speak to it in your private speech. Say:

I ask my higher self to send me vivid images (you can choose thoughts instead of images if you so desire. Simply replace the words "vivid images" with "lucid thoughts") *as to where I will meet my soul mate. The images will start as soon as I reabsorb the sphere.*

Reabsorb the sphere into your crown chakra and breathe

in a 2/4 rhythm. Close your eyes and wait for a minute or so. Your higher self may not answer, especially if you're new to working with it. In that case, repeat the process and ask the *exact same* question. The more you work with it, the easier it gets.

Nick W. came to me with a puzzled look on his face. I asked him what was going on.

He said, "I've tried everything to get a soul mate, but nothing seems to work."

"Maybe the time isn't right," I said to him.

"How can there be a right time and a wrong time?" He asked.

"There are several factors that come into play," I said.

"What factors are those," he wondered.

"You have to be ready for a soul mate. A soul mate is more than just somebody that you love. A soul mate is someone who makes you whole on many levels. You may be ready mentally, but you may not are ready spiritually," I instructed.

"Well how can I get ready?" He wondered.

"You can ask your higher self what is standing in your way of you having a soul mate at this time," I said.

"So let's do it," he replied.

I hypnotized Nick and then asked him to access his higher self. I asked his higher self, "What is blocking Nick from having a soul mate at this time?"

Nick remained still for a moment, and then said, "I'm not emotionally ready for a soul mate."

"What does Nick have to do with his emotions?" I asked.

"I cling to women," he said.

"Emotionally?" I asked.

"Yes," he said.

I brought Nick back into consciousness and asked him about his last relationship.

"I broke up about six months ago. I'm looking for a new relationship. So how do I get on with it?" Nick wrung his hands.

"You have to deal with the issues surrounding your last relationship before you can move onto a new one," I said.

"So what about it?" He asked.

"Why did you break up?" I asked.

Nick sighed, and then said, "Because she said I wouldn't let her go out with her friend."

"And why wouldn't you?" I asked.

"Because I thought the two of them were going to bars and picking up guys," he said.

"This is what you need to work on. This is the lesson you need to learn in order to have a soul mate," I said.

THE SELF

A t the deepest layer of your unconscious lies God within. Jung termed it the Self, but many people in the New Age refer to it as your higher self. The Self is there to lead you to wholeness, *if you will let it.* The Biblical book of *Job* is about a new relationship between God and man—one in which God is in our unconscious minds. God is now both within and without. Anyone wanting to learn more about this should read Jung's *Answer to Job.*

Most people choose to shut the Self out, to instead inflate their ego and make it their god. We see this in the arrogance that plagues our society. People have completely abandoned all concept of karma and falsely believe that what they are doing is right and even justified by God. They fail to realize that they are creating karma that must be repaid. They falsely believe that they act in a vacuum and that nothing will befall them as a consequence of those actions.

The court system is a prime example of such institutional arrogance. According to the law, if you are innocent, then your case is supposed to be dismissed. Judges and prosecutors act "in the interest of society." They justify their actions—up to and including sending an innocent person to prison to cover a mistake—by believing that they are right and doing good. The fact that society backs these people up for such behavior (and even rewards them) only makes the situation worse.

Their egos are so inflated that they justify sending away an innocent man by rationalizing their decision with the falsehood that he probably did something in the past that he got away with. They decide to play God and meed out punishment for karma that may or may not deserve punishment, if it exists at all.

They focus only on this world and its ways, failing to see the big picture. They believe that God will reward them for their actions and that there is nothing more to it. Much of the arrogance in this country stems from this false notion. Jesus said that if you confess, then the slate will be wiped clean. Though the offense has been forgiven, the karma hasn't been erased—the energy of the act must be dealt with. Jesus also said to turn the other cheek and pray for your enemies. He knew that such things would only send the bad acts back upon those who did them.

To shut out the Self to such an extent can result in several lifetimes of repayment. Why would you want to shut out what is urging you to wholeness? The Self is there to assist you, and you can use it to attract your soul mate.

Hunches, images, and fantasies that come to mind for no reason can all come from the Self. They burst into ego consciousness for a reason. Most people dismiss them as nonsense, but the wise man pays attention to them. The ones that repeat time and time again are kicking you in the teeth, trying to get you to pay attention to them.

Begin paying attention to hunches and images that come to mind when you are around people. The more you practice this, the better you'll get at it. Listen to your deeper mind, it is speaking to you, and it is leading you in the right direction. Stop thinking that everything that exists is outside of you. Such a view is atheistic, for it denies the existence of the spirit world and God Himself.

The spring of divine love

True and unconditional love is the love that is the source of all things, and this is the love that makes up the other realm. God Himself is love, and so is everything that you see. Everything is made up of this love energy. God didn't have a pile of material to create from, but rather all He had was energy. Everything can be reduced and measured by the energy that it contains.

There is a way to tap into this love without dying and journeying to the other side. The other side is already inside of you, dwelling within your deeper mind, just waiting for you to tap into it. Most people would dismiss this as utter nonsense or childhood magical thinking, but you must set aside your rational mind and believe.

Do the chakra balancing and surround your body with the sphere of white light as I instructed in the *past life soul mate search* in the last chapter. Now breathe in the 2/4 rhythm and get into a relaxed state.

See a white sphere about the size of a softball coming out of your crown chakra and hovering about a foot above your head. Take a moment to see it glimmer and sparkle with pure white light.

Ask it to wash away your tarnished love. Say:

I ask my higher self to rain on me with the white light of divine and unconditional love. This light washes away any tarnished or corrupt love. It cleanses me of any conditions that I have placed on love along with any resentment or hate that lingers inside of me.

Now see pure white light flowing down from the sphere and raining down on you. See the beam of light flowing as streams of water from a shower. Each beam rolls down your body and is grounded into the earth. You needn't worry because the sphere has an endless supply.

See your tarnished and conditional love being washed away. Any impurity or area that you perceive as black is washed away and replaced with pure white light. Take sufficient time to cleanse yourself.

Now, as the white light continues to rain down upon you, see it filling your body. See your entire body made up of this pure white light. Close your eyes and visualize it. Feel it tingling on the surface of your skin, sensing its warm and tender energy caressing your entire body. Take sufficient time to feel the depth of this.

See the pure white light stop from raining down on you. See the sphere remain there, and thank it for the love that it has showered upon you. Reabsorb the sphere and breathe in a 2/4 rhythm for several moments.

Repeat this ritual at least once a week, perhaps once a day if you are seeking a soul mate. The more filled you are with pure and unconditional love; the easier it will be to attract a soul mate.

D
on't resist this kind of love, and don't con yourself into believing that it only exists in fairy tales. If you settle for conditional love in your thinking--believing that this is all that is possible while locked in a human body--then this is the reality that you will live. If you think that you have to accept any love that is lower than pure and unconditional love, then you have already prepared for this reality to occur. Don't believe it.

Ego-centered, conditional love is a love that is shrinking away from the true love within. Instead of experiencing this divine love, the ego decides to invent its own limited definitions of what unconditional love is. Since the source of true love within is cut off, the ego has nothing to compare its limited thoughts to.

Let go of the ego and its notions about love. Begin to tap into that love that is within, and use it on a daily basis instead of relying on the ego. The best way to go about this is do as Jesus did, to unconditionally love everyone that you come in contact with.

Even if someone is difficult or a jerk, you have a choice in the matter, you can choose to respond out of love. The only way to do this is to let go of the ego and tap into the love that comes from the Self. The minute that you judge or blame, the ego swells and shuts out the Self.

Jim V. came to me and told me that the whole soul mate thing was a joke and that I—and others in the New Age field—were committing an incredible fraud on the public. I asked him to be more specific.

"I've had three 'soul mates' in a row and none of them were hardly divine," he said.

"So what happened?" I asked.

"The first unconditional love relationship that I had was

30

supposedly based on a past life together. She turned out to be a cheating bitch. When she left me she took everything. And just to throw it in my face, she left me one fork, one spoon, and one knife," he huffed.

"I could hypnotize you and bring you back to the cause of why she treated you in this manner. Perhaps there is a legitimate karmic reason for this and if there is, I can help you overcome it," I said.

"Forget your New Age stuff. All this talk is nothing but a bunch of crap," he said with a flush face.

"There may be something in one of your past lives that you need to know," I said.

"I've heard enough of your mumbo jumbo and have bought enough of your books and CDs," he said.

"Tell me about these other women that you also had problems with," I said.

"What about 'em?" He snapped, "They're all the same. There's no such thing as a soul mate."

"Did they leave you as well?" I asked.

"What's it to ya?" He snapped.

"It sounds like there's a karmic pattern here. Perhaps you were cruel to women in a past life," I said.

"Women are a bunch of cruel witches. Every one of them is the same," he said.

"That's not true. The women that you are meeting—," I began.

He interrupted, and said, "Don't give me that stuff. There's no magical solution to all of this."

"But this is a lesson you need to learn," I said.

"And what is that? To only deal in one night stands?" He said in a bitter tone.

"There is something you need to learn about women. Some lesson that has followed you around for several lifetimes," I said.

"Don't con me with your stuff," he said.

"Do you want to overcome this or do you want to meet another woman just like all the rest?" I asked.

He signed boldly, blowing hot air out of his nostrils. He stared at me for a prolonged moment, and then said, "Okay, but this better work."

"It will," I reassured him.

I hypnotized Jim and brought him back to the cause of his problem with women. He lingered in visiting the scene from his past life before he acknowledged that he was doing so.

"Where are you?" I asked.

"It looks like I'm in an Ali Baba movie," he said.

"Ask your higher mind where you are," I instructed.

"I'm in Mecca and the year is 1542," he said.

"What are you doing?" I asked.

"I'm entering my house. I have many wives," he said.

"Do you recognize any of them?" I asked.

"One of them is Betty, and one of them is the woman I just broke up with," he said.

"That's good; this is what you need to see. So what are you doing with your wives?" I asked.

"I'm yelling at a couple of them and ignoring a few others," he said.

"What are they doing?" I asked.

"They are taking care of the household chores. A couple of them are trying to speak to me," he said.

"Why won't you respond to them?" I probed.

"I don't know," he said.

"What are they saying," I asked.

"One is pleading with me to deal with a situation that I don't quite understand. Another one is crying, but I'm ignoring her," he said.

"Try to pinpoint why you are ignoring them," I instructed.

"I don't see them as being equal to men," he said.

"Try to go deeper. See what you're doing," I instructed.

"I think that they are stupid for showing emotion. I am keeping them from fully expressing their emotions by snapping at them," he said.

"And what are they doing?" I asked.

"Some of them are slipping out of the room and pretending to be doing chores when I've got my back turned. Most of them are refusing to look at me and of the ones that are, they are doing so with fear in their eyes and on trembling knees," he said.

I brought Jim back into consciousness. He was unable to look me in the eye, glancing at me fast and in flashes as though he was afraid I was going to snap at him.

"You keep attracting these same women to yourself. They treat you as you have treated them. They are ignoring you emotionally and walking out on you," I said.

"Yeah, so what," he said while staring at his shoes. "It didn't change anything. There still ain't no such thing as soul mates."

"Yes there is. All you have to do is listen to women and be there emotionally for them," I said.

Jim looked up at me with the sense of wonder about his face. He remained frozen for several moments, and then said, "That's exactly what I've been doing."

"You haven't learned that lesson in all these lifetimes. Once you have learned the lesson, you will erase the karma," I said.

I instructed Jim to explore any other past lives that were affecting him today. His mind drifted for some time and then his facial expression changed. I waited a moment, and then asked him, "So where are you?"

"I'm on the prairie sometime during the old west," he said.

"Who are you with?" I asked him.

"Just my wife."

"So tell me about your relationship?"

"There's not much to tell. We just got married and I built us a log cabin."

"So what kind of woman is she?"

"She is fragile and dependent on me. She is six or seven years younger than me. If I wouldn't provide food and water, I don't know what she would do."

"So what happened that led to your current problem with women?"

He sighed boldly, and then replied, "There was this bad storm and part of the roof got torn off. While reaching for the hammer I slipped and fell. I broke my leg bad. My wife patched me up the best that she could and then took off in the wagon to fetch the doctor."

"So what happened?"

"I thought that she would never return but she did the next day."

"And did she bring the doctor with her?" I posed.

"Yes."

"And what happened?"

"While he was setting my leg, she told me that she got lost." He sighed boldly before going on, "I yelled and screamed at her and called her a dumb woman. I kept yelling at her even after she started bawling. I told her that the town only has a few hundred people, that she should've asked for directions, etc. I kept yelling at her even after the doctor said it was enough."

"So what happened?" I posed.

"We struggled during the winter, sometimes going for days without food. My uncle and brother brought wood and food, but they forgot all too often, each one thinking that it was the other's turn. What they did bring was never enough to last until the next one came."

"So what happened with your relationship with your wife?"

He sighed deeply, and then replied, "I turned bitter toward her. I came to believe that I couldn't depend on her for anything. This attitude grew worse over the years. I never let her go into town alone after that."

I brought Jim back into consciousness and he looked at me with a stunned look on his face.

"I keep repeating the same pattern," he gasped.

"And now that you know that, you can finally learn the karmic lesson that you need to learn in order to balance your karma and move on."

I heard from Jim about six months later. He was with a new woman and things couldn't be more different.

A love koan

A man once approached me, and asked, "How come my wife doesn't love me? I buy her all sorts of things."

"Buy her?" I said.

"What do you mean?" He wondered.

"Can things love?" I posed.

"I buy my wife things because I love her. I brought her flowers the other day," he said.

"Do the flowers listen to her?" I asked.

"What are you talking about?" He asked.

"Love, what are you talking about?" I inquired.

"That's what I'm talking about," he said.

"Love must grow up from the earth where it is raised by corporations to be cut, packaged, and sold," I said.

"What are you talking about? I buy my wife flowers because I love her," he said.

"It must be on sale," I said.

"What do you mean?" He looked at me with a perplexed look on his face.

"You buy your wife flowers yet she doesn't love you," I said.

"That's what I asked you half an hour ago," he sighed.

"When she wants a shoulder to cry on or someone to caress her, she finds only flowers," I said.

"So what am I supposed to do? What is the bottom line?" He asked.

"Listen to the flowers," I said.

H ere is a Zen meditation that will give you the answer you need to what is either blocking your relationship or what is blocking you from your soul mate. The way that you need to go will be revealed to you, as will any way that you need a direction for.

Get into a meditative state. See a sphere of pure white light at your crown chakra. Take a few moments to see it pulsate. Now see a map laid out in front of you, seeing the place that you are at on one side of the map. Ask a question about where you need to go; something that is blocking you, etc and you will see where you need to go on the map. You should see a road and an image, which may be symbolic. If you don't understand it or need clarification, then ask the question again.

Jung coined the term synchronicity to describe those rare incidents where inner and outer events correspond. Have you ever had a pre-cognitive dream where all or part of it came true the next day? You were experiencing synchronicity. You need to begin seeing this, to stop thinking that outside is all that exists or is the only place to find anything. Come to see that within and without are one in the same. The Zen meditation in the *Introduction* will help you develop this.

Most people only encounter synchronicity when they are searching for their soul mate. Repressed material from the unconscious can surface in the form of another person. You experience urges, feelings, and have hunches that you have known this person before. The soul mate will seem to be someone that you went to high school with, yet they may have come from thousands of miles away.

Many such events may occur as unconscious material, which the soul mate brings up, and finds its corresponding place outside of you in reality. Events from past lives may thrust into consciousness and connections between events that don't seem to go together will present themselves. They won't make sense until you go back to your past life.

Valerie G. had been living with her current boyfriend Ben for just over three years when she began having problems. She seemed to be fighting with Ben more than usual, which kept them apart from each other. Images surrounding babies and synchronicity plagued her. Once when she was out driving, she stumbled upon a stroller that had been set out for one of the veterans' groups to pick up. She got out of the car to examine it, finding it in perfect working order. She pushed it down the sidewalk with tears streaming down her eyes. Following a few minutes, she folded up the stroller and shoved it into her car. She drove off with it despite the fact that one of the neighbors was watching her.

"So why did you drive off with the stroller?" I asked her.

"Because it struck something deep within me. It was so powerful that I just couldn't resist. I had to do it," she said.

"So what was going on inside of you that struck such a nerve?" I asked.

"The image of me pushing a baby in a stroller came up from my unconscious mind right before I happened upon the stroller. It was vivid. It was a perfect spring day, the sun was shining, the baby was smiling and giggling, and a woman was hanging laundry on a line," she said.

"Were you thinking anything that may have provoked this image to come to mind?" I asked.

"*No, I wasn't even thinking about babies,*" she said almost defensively.

"So what's the deal with babies?" I asked her.

She opened her mouth to say something, but her lips stammered. Her voice broke, resulting in a gurgling sound coming from deep within her throat. She inhaled hard, breaking into a fit of tears that lasted longer than a moment, and then took a deep breath. She waited several minutes before she was ready to say something. She said, "All my life I wanted to have a baby and be a mother. When I was a little girl, I even named my dolls."

"So what happened?" I asked her.

She broke into tears, which she choked back fast. She wiped each eye and then said without looking at me, "I can't have a baby. We've tried everything and have been to every fertility doctor on Earth, but it just wasn't meant to be."

"Perhaps there is something from one of your past lives that is preventing you from becoming a mother. I could regress you. We might find something of use," I said.

"I might as well. I've tried everything else," she said.

I hypnotized Valerie and brought her back to the Middle Ages, back to a time when England was steeped in cruelty and the plague. She found herself working as a maid for a wealthy family. She was married, but she didn't have any children. Her husband worked for the same family, performing a series of different jobs, but worked largely in the stables and as a blacksmith.

"So where are you now?" I asked her.

"I'm sorting sheets to be washed. Several large pots sit on fires. They are filled with soapy water and are used to get the sheets clean. The lady of the house likes the laundry to be spotless. She considers even a spec of dirt to be an abomination against God," she said.

"So what's happening now? Describe what you see," I instructed her.

"I'm getting ready to put some sheets in a pot when the lady of the house comes up to me. I gasped and dropped the sheet that I am holding," she said.

"What made you react like that?" I probed.

"The lady of the house almost never comes down to where the laundry is being done. I felt my heart racing in my chest, bracing my self to be yelled at. She stood there staring at me for what seemed like forever. I felt my knees buckling and I thought that I was going to collapse," she said.

"Is your husband there? Is anybody else there?" I asked.

"No. There were a few other women standing around, but I think they hightailed it," she said.

"So what is the lady of the house doing?" I asked.

"She asks me if I am pregnant," she said and then gasped.

"Describe exactly what you feel and tell me what's going on," I instructed her.

"I'm shivering from head to toe. I want to pee, but I have to hold it back. The lady of the house told me in a firm voice when I was hired that it wasn't proper for a woman to have a baby unless the husband could provide a house for the family. I told her that I didn't think that I was pregnant, but I could be. She said that if I became pregnant, I had to leave the house immediately. I wet myself because I was two weeks late with my period," she said.

"Okay, I want you to move forward in time. Move to a point where you find out whether you're pregnant or not. Can you see it?" I asked.

"Yes, it's about three months in the future," she said.

"Describe everything that is happening," I instructed.

"I wore baggy dresses and concealed my stomach long enough. The lady of the house caught me in a lie and ordered me to pull my dress up. When she saw my stomach, she ordered me to pack up my things and leave the house at once. I pleaded with tears streaming down my eyes. I screamed out at the top of my lungs, '*I'm married. I'm married.*' The lady of the house made me feel like a knocked up slut," she said.

Valerie, despite being married, had to leave that city. She lived in a barn with her husband where he worked as a blacksmith. She didn't get a room of her own until just before the baby came. She didn't get a house in that lifetime.

In her current incarnation, Valerie found herself in the same situation. Though she was married, she lived in an apartment with her husband. The building manager was a woman. Several months later, she managed to get pregnant, although she remained in her apartment.

DON'T MARRY YOUR MOTHER

Most of us unconsciously seek the same qualities in a mate as those in the parent of the opposite sex, and we don't know that we're doing it. We can end up marrying our mother instead of our soul mate, and miss out on the spiritual development that we were supposed to get. Many of these archetypes can give us false feelings and other indications that this person is the one that we are supposed to be with. It is important that we understand these archetypes, including how to separate them from those unconscious contents that are leading us to our soul mates.

We attract to ourselves, largely in an unconscious sense, the same qualities and habits that exist in the parent of the opposite sex. Women are attracted to men who wear the same cologne that their fathers wore. Scientific studies have found that similar body odors, including a hint of urine, all figure into a woman's choice of a mate.

You can't continue to be so oblivious to this, you must make it conscious. Be aware that you are doing this. Pay attention when you are dating. Many women unconsciously pick up on things in their mate, picking them up psychically as well. A woman will set up the same situation that she had with her father. If he died suddenly of a heart attack at the age of 57, she will unconsciously pick a man who has a good chance of dying of a heart attack in his fifties. You psychically pick up on many other things about your mate without being consciously aware of it.

We all have an unconscious script, which is based on our experiences growing up as a child, of what sort of married life we want. This is more visible, i.e. conscious, in women. Women have this idealized vision of the house, the husband, and how many children they want, etc, well mapped out in their heads. The male vision usually revolves around money and a job, but they have a more flexible vision of the house and kids.

If you're not aware that you have this script planted in your unconscious, then you may be reacting to it like a zombie. A woman may choose someone who resembles her father or even has her father's mannerisms. She will more than likely, albeit largely unconsciously, get a sense of security and comfort from this.

If you want to find your soul mate, then you must be aware of this script. The best way to go about it is to be aware of the qualities in the parent of the opposite sex and the circumstances of your childhood. The woman will especially try to recreate what she had as a child with her own children. Watch for the regular patterns that you fall into regarding this, and then step outside of them and go forth in a new direction.

We all have within us, locked deep in our unconscious minds, a mother archetype. This will usually make its presence known by recurring images and thoughts that thrust them into consciousness. These images may be of your own mother or they may be of a mother figure. They could be of nurturing things such as food, the house that you grew up in as a child, your teddy bear, etc.

The mother archetype can also take on dark and sinister undertones. The nagging voice of your own mother, which can be your own voice in your private speech, but definitely your mother's words, is a common archetype of the mother. This voice is usually associated with guilt, and is brought on when you are going beyond what your mother told you to do.

Many people project the mother archetype onto other people, especially onto a mate. We unconsciously seek someone who will set those same barriers in place for us, and make us feel guilty when we step over them. In a more sinister and self-destructive form, we seek out someone who will make us do things that we don't want to do. Such a dark mother archetype seeks to destroy us instead of nurture us.

If you want to find your soul mate, then it is best that you free yourself from the mother archetype. In order to have a soul mate, you may need to transcend the limits that exist in your mind or find nurturing in a new way. The old ways aren't going to work for you. They're only going to keep you locked in the lower levels of consciousness.

Uprooting the mother archetype

In order to remove anything from your reality, you have to first pluck it from your unconscious mind. With an unconscious that is no longer holding you back, your consciousness will expand to include a soul mate. Within and without are one thing, not two separate things. Coming to understand and accept this will greatly help you.

Do the chakra balancing and protection technique that I have explained in the *past life soul mate search* in *The nature of soul mates* chapter. Breathe in the 2/4 rhythm—inhale for a count of 2, hold your breath for a moment, and then exhale for a count of 4. Take a few minutes to get into a relaxed state.

See a white sphere about the size of a softball coming out of your crown chakra and hovering about a foot above your head. Take a moment to see it pulsate with pure white light.

Now is the time for you to change what needs to be changed. You should have made a list before you started this ritual of the images and thoughts of the mother archetype and what qualities of the parent of the opposite sex that you no longer want to attract—both consciously and unconsciously.

Say the following, making sure that you add nothing more than your own qualities in the areas indicated. See the words going into the sphere and becoming part of it. Say:

I now seek to let go of the past and to release my old ways of doing things. I now release my unconscious attraction to the parent of the opposite sex. I no longer seek the same qualities in potential mates and lovers that I see in this parent. I release the desire to seek someone who has the same health problems as my father, (add your own here). *I release also my mother archetype, its images, and unconscious entities. I release the recurring image and the entities that stand behind the guilt that my mother laid on me,* (add your own here).

When you have finished, take a moment to see the sphere glistening with white light. Reabsorb the sphere into your crown chakra, knowing that it is a seed that will be planted in your unconscious mind. Anything that is planted in the field of the unconscious will eventually become reality.

Now breathe in the 2/4 rhythm, and keep going until you are in a relaxed state. Take a few minutes and sit there, knowing that the seed that you have planted is growing at that moment.

You may have to repeat the above ritual more than once in order to root out all of the crap that has been planted in your mind.

Rikki W. had grown up in a stormy environment that centered on her alcoholic father. Her mother, who often fought with her father, could never bring herself to file for divorce. Her father refused to go to Alcoholics Anonymous (AA) meetings and would leave the house for a bar if her mother so much as mentioned it.

Years later, Rikki's father passed away. Rikki went away to college and fell for a much older man. The man, though successful and earning an above average paycheck, had a severe drinking problem. It was several months into her marriage that Rikki came to me.

"What's going on?" I asked her.

"I keep trying to get Lou to go to AA, but he won't go," she said.

"You knew that he had a substantial drinking problem when you married him. Why didn't you sober him up before you married him?" I asked.

"I thought that I could change him if I made him a married man." She wiped her eyes.

"That's a common fallacy among women. Men are more realistic. They know that a woman will be pretty much the same even after they are married. But a woman thinks that she can turn any man into a Ken doll," I said.

"I know. But what can I do now? Is there something from one of my past lives that got me into this situation?" She wiped her eyes once again.

"Maybe there is and maybe there isn't. If there is, it probably has to do with your father," I said.

"I've been struggling with this whole past life connection for sometime," she said.

"You married Lou because you were unconsciously attracted to the same qualities in him that existed in your father," I suggested.

"Maybe you're right," she said.

"Your father died suddenly, which complicated the matter. Your desires to turn Lou into the ideal husband are an unconscious attempt to save your father," I said.

Her facial expression changed, and her mouth hung open. She said following a moment, "Oh my God, you're right!"

"Lou might not even be your soul mate. It might be that you're not even supposed to be with him. You could be unfolding in a direction that you weren't supposed to go," I said.

Rikki cried and then her voice broke as she tried to say something. She said, "I'm pregnant with his child. I can't just leave him."

"And did you think that this would make him a good father?" I asked.

Rikki burst into tears and then said in a voice that was barely audible, "Yes."

"You can't save your father. He died an alcoholic and there's nothing that you can do to change that. You have to let go

45

of him. Not only on a conscious level, but on an unconscious level as well," I said.

"That's great to know. What good does it do me now?" She cried.

"You know the truth. You know that the men that you choose are based on the qualities in your father, the ones that were the most emotional and the most painful. You have to let go of this," I said.

"It would be easier without the baby," she said.

Rikki had a baby boy about seven months later, and it didn't result in Lou abandoning the bottle. I taught Rikki how to be aware of her unconscious script surrounding her father and how to release it. I wanted to regress her to see if there was a past life that was influencing this situation. After some reluctance on her part, and two cancellations, she agreed to undergo regression. I put her under and then instructed her, "I want you to go back to the past life that is most influencing your present situation."

She paused for a moment, and then replied, "I'm seeing horses…and people."

"Focus in on it. Where are you?"

"Someplace ancient. People are dressed like Ancient Greece…yes, it is Greece."

"And what are you doing?"

"I'm picking grapes on my family vineyard along with my father, brothers, sisters, and some hired hands."

"Where is your mother?"

Her voice broke when she said, "She…died several years earlier from some sort of virus during the winter."

"And how old are you?"

"I think around nine or ten."

"And what is your relationship with your father?"

"I'm the youngest and I won't let my father out of my sight."

"And how is your relationship with your siblings?"

Her gazed lowered, and then she said, "It's not so good. They pick on me a lot because I'm the youngest. We fight a lot more since mom died. My dad can't handle us like mom used to."

"So describe your relationship with your father to me?"

"There's not much more to say."

"Did anything significant happen between you and your father?"

She gulped, pausing for a little longer than a moment, and then responded, "He was close to forty years old and he was pushing himself to get the grapes picked because it was our only source of income. He was picking up a basket that was overloaded with grapes when he doubled over in pain and clutched his chest." She started to cry, "By the time I got to him he was unconscious."

"So what were you feeling at that moment?" I posed.

"I felt that I was alone in the world and that I would have to beg for crumbles in the street." She cried even harder.

I waited for a moment, and then asked, "So what happened to your father?"

"He regained consciousness, but he was weak. I think he had a mild heart attack. He could never work in the fields again. He was weak and he had trouble catching his breath at times."

"So what happened after that? Did your father recover some of his strength?" I questioned.

"No, he got worse little by little. I cared for him and brought him food, but the more attention I gave him, the worse he got."

"So what happened to him?"

"He died a few years later. I was raised by an aunt with one of my sisters and the rest of my siblings were split up."

I brought Rikki back into consciousness. She instantly knew why she was clinging to the father archetype and seeking the same qualities that were in her mate as the qualities that were in her father.

After much soul searching, Rikki left Lou. She dated a couple of men since and has been working to find her soul mate.

Jung developed the concept of the anima and animus, the masculine and the feminine aspects of our personalities. We all have both of these in our unconscious minds, but we may be more in touch with one than the other. Thus, some men are macho while others are rather feminine. The same is true for women. Some women are business leaders and others are suited to be stay at home mothers.

The anima is the eternal image of women in us all, comprising the feminine aspect of our personalities. This isn't the image of any woman in particular, but a universal image of women as a whole. The anima can appear in dreams, fantasies, and images that spontaneously arise from the unconscious, and even as the nagging voice of your mother.

The animus is just the opposite, the eternal image of men in all of us. The animus is most clearly visible in women who project it onto strong men—jocks, firemen, writers, etc.

The anima/animus most clearly manifests in dreams and fantasies as the dream lover. We all have this image of an ideal lover, someone that we want to be with and cuddle with. We need to pay attention to this lover. What qualities does the lover have? Why are you attracted to this person? What do you want them to do for you? What needs do you want them to fulfill?

Someone with a gorgeous dream lover might have an unfulfilled need for attention or to possess good looks. Someone who has a dream lover with large breasts might have an unfulfilled need to be mothered. The qualities in the dream lover may be qualities that are lacking in us, or they may be unconscious complexes that we need to deal with. This is why you need to carefully examine these fantasies.

The anima/animus functions as a buffer between the outside world and us. They are a layer between our thoughts about a dream lover and our actual lover, which can either help or hurt our relationship. The images of the dream lover help us deal with a less than perfect lover or they can cause us to reject our lover and seek an illicit affair. If we are to find our soul mate, we must rid ourselves of the dark aspects of the anima and animus.

We must be aware of the fact that we unconsciously project the anima or animus onto our lover. Every woman wants some kind of hero—a pro athlete, fireman, top executive, etc. Every man wants a woman that other men will be envious of—a beauty queen, centerfold, model, etc. We must stop projecting this onto our lovers and accept our lovers as they are. Let go of the notions of ideals, heroes, models, etc. Come to see that the qualities that you are projecting onto your lover are actually inside yourself. A woman who pushes her husband to be a superjock often has a repressed wish to be recognized, brave, or strong.

What is absent in your outer attitude will be found in your inner attitude. Thus someone who is weak or timid will have a brave anima/animus. You are not the same person as the person that you show to the world. You're just the opposite. The only problem is that the inner you is largely unconscious and inaccessible to an ego that inflates and limits itself.

Go back to the *uprooting the mother archetype* and repeat the technique. Add the following after the first two paragraphs:

Release the belief that I am identical with my persona, outer attitude. Never transfer the images from my anima or animus to anther person.

Anima/animus awareness

The best way not to be influenced by the anima/animus when making your soul mate choice is to be aware of them. Breathe in a 2/4 rhythm and bring on a relaxed state. Close your eyes and visualize yourself on a beach. The sun is shining and a gentle breeze caresses your face. You are alone, seeing nothing but undisturbed sand from horizon to horizon.

See someone approaching you from the end of the beach. You can't make them out at first but then they come into view. The person is your dream lover, the one that you have fantasized about your entire life. As this person approaches you, take the time to examine every detail of their being. Try to see what stands out and whether or not the person has any imperfections.

See the person walk up to you, taking your hand. The two of you sit down on a blanket together. The person speaks to you in a loving voice. What do they say? What does their voice sound like? Take a few minutes to soak in every detail.

Now return to consciousness and open your eyes. You have just met your anima or animus. Write down all the qualities, imperfections, and any impressions that you gathered. You will see that many of these things are the opposite of what you are. You will discover you.

Dwayne L. had always been attracted to large breasted women and his second wife had 54 GGs. Though he believed he was involved in a relationship that other men should envy, there were times when it was hard to hold it together. At one time it became so bad that Betty packed up and went to her mother's house. It was at this point that he contacted me for advice.

"So what happened that made Betty pack up and leave?" I asked.

Dwayne sighed boldly, and then said, "She said that I was acting like an infant."

"And were you?" I posed.

"Not really…I don't think so," he said.

"Think so," I said.

Dwayne sighed, and then said without looking at me, "She said that I spend too much time playing with her breasts."

"And do you?" I asked.

Dwayne sighed, and then said, "I guess I do."

"So did you marry a woman or a pair of breasts?" I posed.

"I would probably have to say that I married a nice pair of

tits," he said.

"So what do you find so fascinating about breasts?" I asked.

"They're so big. I want everybody to see me with them," he said.

"And what do they symbolize to you?" I asked.

"I'm not sure what you mean," he said.

"Do you want to be mothered?" I asked.

"No." He looked at me with a puzzled look.

"Do you want big breasts or some other feature for people to notice?" I asked.

"It isn't breasts," he said.

"So you're attracted to women with big breasts because you have a small penis?" I asked.

He looked at me for a few moments without saying anything.

I waited several minutes, giving him ample time to answer. I said, "Don't you see what you've been doing? You're using big breasts to compensate for your small penis. The large breasts are a visible symbol of what is small and hidden."

"So what should I do, buy a penis pump?" He said.

"Or better yet, become aware of your inner attitude and anxieties concerning such. As long as the attitude remains unconscious, you will have this problem."

Dwayne and Betty broke up not long after he spoke to me. Since he became aware of what he was doing, he quit trying to compensate for his small penis. Several months later, he began dating a woman with average sized breasts who was much more suited to him.

51

THE ALCHEMY OF SOUL MATES

Jung studied alchemy for many years and discovered that what the alchemists were really working with was not mystical chemistry experiments, but the workings of the unconscious mind. The alchemists of the Middle Ages proved to be just as accurate at describing the workings of the unconscious mind as the psychologists of the twentieth century. The field of alchemy was ripe for study and rebirth, but this time by psychologists.

What the alchemists said about the mixing of metals was really going on in their own minds. By trying to join opposite metals, sulfur and mercury, they believed that they could make gold or silver. What they really discovered was what Jung discovered several centuries later—that the union of opposites leads to wholeness. This is no more true than in balancing karma, which requires that you go through what you have put out.

The union of opposite partners leads to wholeness as well, but this wholeness has more than one element to it. The union of soul mates has a spiritual aspect to it that not only connects us to the self, but it connects us to the past lives of our partner as well. When the two soul mates come together, they become much more than the two halves, and more than two bodies involved in a single life time.

Alchemists described this union as that of the sun and the moon or sulfur and mercury. They saw it as not merely the joining of two metals, but the joining of natures. Finding a soul mate is a spiritual experience, one that heightens your own connection with God. And this is supposed to happen, for if it doesn't, you haven't found your soul mate.

Your nature involves who you are, who you really are and not the mask that you wear for society. You can't be phony or put on some sort of lounge lizard routine if you want a soul mate. So many of us have become our workday personas that we don't know who the real us is any more. We've become plastic and artificial, trading a sense of wonder for the security of a paycheck.

Your nature will blend with your soul mate's nature, often in ways that aren't so obvious. We've all seen an attractive woman with an average looking man and have wondered what she sees in him. Beauty is in the eye of the beholder. She might see in him what we don't see just by looking at him, what is beyond mere surface beauty.

When you join with your soul mate, your consciousness expands. The other opposite, once united, will expand your awareness and increase your understanding. You will see things, and not just those that concern your mate, in a light that you haven't seen them in before. They were always there, but you didn't possess the awareness to see them.

This joining—what the alchemists called conituncito—has a transforming effect on both soul mates. The nature that you had going in will be changed and who you are will be forever altered. The two base metals will become fine gold, many parts of it becoming even stronger then they once were.

When you are joined with your soul mate, every aspect of you is joined. So don't discount the lesser aspects of yourself because they also have value. Your weakness, which many need to grow and be the very reason you came together with your soul mate, may become your strengths.

The alchemists of old used various symbols to describe this union of opposites. The most noted were the sun and moon, as was sulfur and mercury. The sun and moon hermaphrodite was a common symbol of the united opposites. It is shown with sun (male) and moon (female) heads atop a single body. The hermaphrodite is a symbol of an encounter with the Self, often depicted as the God within.

Discover your mercury element

In order to find your soul mate, you have to find out what nature in you needs to be developed. You have to be honest with yourself about who you are and what your nature is. You also have to be honest with yourself about what needs to be developed and why.

Do the *anima/animus awareness* that I described in the last chapter and find the qualities that are opposite of you. Give some thought to each one, and come up with a list of qualities about yourself. These may be things that you don't like or want to face, but it is important that you not only face them, but put them on the list as well.

Now do the chakra balancing and protection. Breathe in the 2/4 rhythm and take a few minutes to get into a relaxed state. See a white sphere about the size of a softball coming out of your crown chakra and hovering about a foot above your head. Take a minute or so to see it sparkling with pure, white light.

Now take out your list of qualities. Say the following, seeing the words go into the sphere:

I ask my higher self what nature I need to develop concerning (state the quality). *My higher self will send me vivid images* (or lucid thoughts if you prefer) *now.*

Wait for an answer, you should get one. I want you to work with your higher self because the more that you work with it, the easier it will be, and the more readily it will assist you without being asked. If you don't get an answer after two minutes, try it again.

Now I want you to ask it another question, and once again see it going into the sphere:

I ask my higher self what holes need to be filled concerning (state the quality). *My higher self will send me vivid images* (or lucid thoughts if you prefer) *now.*

Once you have exhausted all of the qualities, wait and see if you get an answer. If you don't, try again.

When you have finished with each quality, take a moment to see if there is an overall pattern. The pattern will usually be something rather broad such as a need to learn to let go, a need to trust your partner, etc.

Now breathe in the 2/4 rhythm. Thank your higher self for its guidance and then reabsorb the sphere into your crown chakra. Breathe in the 2/4 rhythm for another minute or so, bringing on a relaxed state.

Cecilia P. had been living with Chuck for over two years when she began to encounter friction in her relationship. The problem simmered, showing no sign of going away. It was when her mother-in-law figured into the situation that she came to me for help.

"So what's going on with your mother-in-law?" I asked her.

"It's this whole Catholic thing. I tried and tried, but I'm just not a Catholic. The harder she pushes, the more I resist," she said.

"Didn't they know about your New Age beliefs?" I asked.

She gazed down at her shoes and gulped. She said, "Not really." She paused for a moment, and then said, "I never could bring myself to tell them."

"And what about Chuck?" I asked.

"He hasn't told his parents anything. They still think he's Catholic," she said.

"Does he go to mass every Sunday?" I asked.

"Not every Sunday, but enough so that his parents see him there every once in awhile," she said.

"So he's putting on a false front for his parents," I said.

"It would be okay with most parents but his parents are so involved with the Catholic Church that it isn't even close to being funny. His parents are always nagging us about getting married and his mom is always pushing Mary on me. I'm really turned off by the whole Mary thing—the statues, the rosary, the works," she said.

"So why don't you tell her that?" I suggested.

"*Are you for real?* That woman would blow a vein out the side of her head," she said.

"Does she frighten you?" I asked.

"There is no way that I can tell this woman about my past lives," she said.

"I think that you should tell her," I said.

"*Are you on drugs? There is no way I can tell her that.* She would probably blame me for Chuck's involvement in the New Age and yank him away from me. I couldn't bare the thought of never seeing Chuck again," she said.

"Then you better buy a rosary and a statue of Mary," I suggested.

"Don't even kid me about that," she huffed.

"You can't go around pretending to be someone that you're not," I said.

"You don't know Chuck's family," she said.

"You have to be who you are. You can't go on wearing a mask just to please other people," I said.

"I can't do it." She wrung her hands; "I can't take a chance at losing Chuck. His mom would yank him back so hard and force him to go to church everyday. I wouldn't even know who he was," she said.

"But it could likely set him free," I said.

"No, I can't chance it." She wrung her hands and fidgeted in her seat.

"Then your only other choice is to wear a bigger mask. That mask will become heavier and require increasing amounts of your psychic energy," I said.

"There's something else that you don't know about," she said and then swallowed hard.

"What is that?" I asked.

"I'm working part-time as a stripper. There's no way that I can tell her this, not on top of reincarnation and everything else," she said.

"See, your mask is getting heavier," I said.

"Well, it's just going to have to get heavier because there's nothing I can do about it," she said.

"This is what's coming between Chuck and you. You have to be honest with each other and be who you are. Instead, you spend all of your psychic energy trying to maintain an image of something that you're not," I said.

"Well, I don't see what else I can do," she said.

"This situation might have an origin in a past life. I think that you should undergo regression and check it out."

"Anything to get out of this mess."

I regressed Cecilia two days later. She wasn't expecting to gain any insight into her situation with her in-laws, but I was convinced that there was at least one past life that figured into this situation. The Catholic Church was just too strong to be an isolated event.

I put Cecilia under and instructed her to go back to the past life that was most affecting her current incarnation. It didn't take her long to find her way. I asked, "So where are you?"

"Somewhere in Medieval Europe. I'm not sure what the date is," she replied.

"The date isn't important. So what are you doing?"

"I'm a nun and I'm wearing a heavy habit. I'm uncomfortable in it because it is a rather warm day, but I simply must wear it."

"And what are you doing?"

"I'm in a rather large building. I don't know if it's a convent or cathedral. Perhaps that convent is part of the cathedral."

"Okay. And what are you doing?"

"I am walking with a group of other nuns. We are going to morning prayers. A man rushes up to us. The nuns scurry out of their organized line and the corridor is filled with tense chatter."

"Is the man a priest?"

"I don't know who he is."

"So what's happening now?" I probed.

"He grabs me by the hand. I let out a shriek and fear for my life. He tells me that it is my sister and to come quick. I ask if she is all right and he just yanks me by the arms and orders me to go with him."

"So what happens next?"

"My feet don't move at first, but his yanking gets them to move. I can hear the chatter from the other nuns and overhear a snide remark or two about me."

"So where does he take you?"

"He takes me outside to a courtyard. An Inquisitor has four women in a row and all of them are bound. Men are preparing stakes for them to be burned. As I looked them over, my heart sank down into the pit of my belly. I feel faint and want to sit down."

"What is making you feel this way?"

"One of the women is my sister. Oh my God! She's my mother-in-law in this life!"

"Why do they have her bound? Do you know what is going on?"

"No, I don't. I rush forward and ask the Inquisitor. He tells me that she is a witch and she has been caught in the act of casting a spell. I tell him that it is impossible. He points to a large wooden box and I see some of my sister's things in there. He says that her diary is a spell book. I plead with him and tell him that it isn't true. I beg for mercy in Christ's name. He finally gave into my pleading and snatched my sister's diary from out of the box. He opened it and shoved it in my face. He said, 'Look there. Shut up.'"

"So what was in the diary?"

"I pulled it from my face. My heart was racing. My nose was still sore. As I pulled the book away, I saw pentagrams in my sister's handwriting. I read it and indeed it was a spell. I flipped through it and found page after page of spells. Tears came to my eyes, tears so strong that I couldn't even see. I dropped the book and approached my sister."

"What was she doing? Was she looking at you?"

"Yes, she was. And when I looked at her, she didn't seem to have a soul. I ask her why? Why? Why? Over and over again. She just stands there staring at me with that stone face. A man with a spear orders me away. I see that the stakes are ready and men with torches are standing at the ready to ignite them. They bring the women forward one by one. I can't bear to watch so I run away in tears."

I brought Cecilia back into consciousness and she quickly realized the forces that were at play here. To admit the truth and "show her the spell book" would result in a "burning at the stake."

Cecilia never could bring herself to tell her in-laws who she really was. As a result, she broke up with Chuck just over a year later.

The Fertility Principle is an expression of the philosopher's stone, a stone that alchemists believed would change base metals into gold. The stone, a symbol of the Self, is the source of psychic energy. It was this energy that the alchemists were really dealing with. By trying to turn lead into gold, they were really trying to craft raw psychic energy into something tangible.

Sex is an expression of psychic energy, one of many avenues that it finds an outlet in. Ancient art is filled with symbols of the penis and the breasts. Images of big breasts and large, erect penises are imprinted onto our minds, being potent symbols of the fullness of the sexual expression of psychic energy.

Many people desire enhancement of the sexual parts of their bodies, and billions are spent on these pursuits. We actually believe that these people have better sex, bigger orgasms, and more lovers than mere mortals.

These things are only *symbols* of the psychic energy that flows from inside of us. Thus, someone who really carves a large penis has a lot of psychic energy that is finding an outlet in sex. Psychic energy can express itself in anything—art, music, athletics, workaholism, etc.

The color green and vegetation are also symbols of the fertility principle. It is common for a man to plant a tree after he has impregnated his wife. The ancient Druids have a specific rite for this, one said to insure an easy birth. A man who gets his wife pregnant will often have dreams of planting a seed, a newly spouted tree, etc.

The fertility principle is at work in soul mates. A good part of this psychic energy is coming from our past lives, thrusting itself into consciousness the first time that you gaze into your soul mate's eyes. Though few people understand this and love's blinding effect can keep anyone from looking beyond their eyes. This is why most soul mates make love more often than most people do.

Psychic energy can find expression in things that you never dreamt of before. Repressed talents and likes from past lives can take a central position in your life once again, though most of them will be somewhat rusty. There are cases of people who have artistic or musical talents at an early age for no apparent reason. These talents were developed in a past life, or perhaps several.

It is best not to try and block or repress this psychic energy, but to let it naturally express itself. Many people panic as they fall head over heels in love and psychic energy overwhelms them, but this will only lead to problems later on. They have been conditioned to believe that frequent lovemaking or what they are feeling is sinful or wrong. They respond to their conditioning that tells them what they should be feeling instead of focusing on what they really are feeling. Let go and be free.

Letting go of your sulfur element
In order to proceed into the future, you must let go of the baggage of the past. We cling, both consciously and unconsciously, to events from the past. The more painful they are, the more power they hold over you. Most of us don't even know that we are doing this, but we feel that something is holding us back. This block is usually blamed on someone else, but blaming someone else only serves to make things even worse.

The pain and memories of a lover that jilted you can be deep-rooted and very powerful. Unless you uproot these and weed them out, they will stand in your way of finding true and lasting love. Few people ever bother with such things, probably because so few of us know how to do it.

The first thing you need to do is make a list of what you need to let go of. Explore the conscious mind, pondering past relationships and anything else that is still painful to you. If you have undergone past life regression and know about your past lives and how they are still affecting you, you can include this material as well.

Next, you need to search your unconscious mind to find the things that are still in the dark. Use the technique that I described in *Discover your mercury element*. Only this time, I want you to ask your higher self what you need to let go of. Wait for a reply. You may have to repeat your request, but this is okay. Once you have gotten the first answer, ask it what else that you need to let go of. Ask this question several times, continuing to a point where you feel you can no longer get an answer.

Reabsorb the sphere and then take a break. Come back sometime later. Do the chakra balancing and protection. Breathe in a 2/4 rhythm, get in a relaxed state, and see the white sphere coming out of your crown chakra. Now take your list of things. Say to the sphere, and see the words going into the sphere:

I release from my unconscious mind, including all emotions, images, and memories of (state one of the things from your list that you need to let go of).

Repeat the above for each of the things that you need to let go of. Reabsorb the sphere and breathe in a 2/4 rhythm until you bring about a relaxed state. Repeat this once a week until you experience some relief from the things that are plaguing you.

Since this stuff is so deep rooted and powerful, there is one more technique that I want you to practice. Get your list of things that you need to let go of. Focus on the first one. It is important that you hold the image of it in your mind. The images are the gateway to the pain and emotions, and you can't release them as long as the image remains in place.

As you hold the image of what you need to let go of in your mind, I want you to breathe deeply at a constant rhythm, but not fast enough to wear you out. This will drain the energy from the emotions behind the pain. As you breathe, tell your unconscious mind to release it. Take at least a couple of minutes on each one.

Here is a metaphysical technique that was used by Druids that will release the emotional pain of a past relationship and let go of an old flame. It was kept secret by the elders and taught only to those who had been initiated when they were ready. It is best to go into the woods or to surround yourself with a plant or two. Light a white candle and meditate on the flame for a few moments. Say *I honor the wise ones of the forest and the trees that they protect.* Stand facing north and bow in that direction. Say *I honor the north.* Go around clockwise and bow in each of the other three directions and do the same thing. Now bow over the spot that you are going to meditate in and say *I honor my ancestors.* Sit down and get into a deep meditative state. See yourself in the scene with the person that is causing you the most pain. Visualize this as clearly as you can. Now see an umbilical cord going between you and him. Now take a pair of scissors and cut the cord. Now see yourself in a new scene. See yourself as you would be if you were *already free of him.* This is important. You have to see yourself as already free of him and not as becoming free of him. In this way, your mind will accept it as true. This is an ancient Druid secret. Now visualize all the little details of yourself being free of him. Feel the joy that you will feel, see the things that you will do, the people that you will hang with, and every detail that goes with it. See how people react to you. Visualize several scenes like this. Do this everyday for 10 to 15 minutes.

YOUR FAMILY WAS DESTINED

You aren't coming together with your soul mate just to party; there is a much higher plan at work here. Many people have embraced the notion that things just happen, that you are born into a certain family at random, and that there is no rhyme or reason as to why you will have the children that you do. Christianity offers no explanation for these things.

Some couples aren't able to have children and this is no accident. One, or both, of the partners committed an act in a past life that led to this situation. They may have stolen someone else's baby and thus are now learning what it is like to be without a child. Unless the karma involved is understood, the reason the couple is infertile will always remain a mystery.

The things you thought were hidden and left behind in your past lives will come to life again in your children. Couples with an autistic child kicked a child around in a past life, thus they now have a child that they must take care of, which they didn't do in their previous incarnation. The autistic child will take away the time from them that they took away from the child that they kicked around in their previous incarnation. Everything balances out and you won't get away with anything.

How much your baby cries is related to karma and what you did in your past lives. Your baby will cry more because it wants to be soothed, which is the direct result of you not soothing your child in a past life. Whenever you think *why is this happening to me* or *this doesn't happen to other people,* what you are really dealing with is karma. You needn't ask God, or blame anyone, but merely examine your past lives because you did it to yourself.

The way that your baby plays is also no accident. If your child wants to be near you when it plays, or constantly watches you while it is playing, it is because you neglected a child in a past life. Now you are being given an opportunity to balance your karma. This also goes for how fast you respond to your child when it cries. Once again, you are being given an opportunity to make up for what you did in the past and balance your karma.

The fundamentalist family who has a pothead son, one that likes to listen to heavy metal music at top volume, will turn to the Bible for answers. Christianity offers no explanation for such things, telling the parents to turn the matter over to God, to pray, etc. While these things are useful, none of them are going to change the karma involved here. The parents need to look at themselves and their past actions and not to outside events as being the cause of such things. It is only with proper understanding, and knowledge of their past lives, that the reason they had a pothead son will come to light.

The family turns to the church for solutions to their son. They believe that their son "doesn't have Jesus in him," and that "finding Jesus," even by force, will turn their son away from pot and back onto the faith. Jesus becomes a magical solution. They try to force their son to attend church, to go to Bible study, attend various church events, trade his heavy metal for Jesus music, etc. In the end, the more force they use, the greater their son will resist, and the louder he will crank the Led Zeppelin CDs.

A family that has a gay son or daughter will think that there is something "wrong" with their child or that they have done something "wrong" in raising the child. They push and prod their child to date members of the opposite sex. If the child is male, they push him to be overtly manly, to play football, etc. If the truth be known, many past NFL greats were secretly gay. They will continue to grasp at such straws because they don't understand the karmic forces at work here or what caused them.

Meditation to find the origin

There is a way to find out what is really going on and the forces that are at play here. You need to first get into a meditative state. See a sphere of pure white light at your crown chakra. Take

66

a few moments to see it pulsate. Now see yourself standing in front of a mirror, watching your crown chakra pulsate in the reflection for a moment. See yourself walking into a house. Now stare into the mirror and you will see the true cause of why you had the child that you did.

Lonnie and Sharon had been married for five years when they had their first child, a son. It wasn't long after they got their son home that they knew there was something seriously wrong with him. He cried almost constantly and always wanted to be held. The doctors told them that he would grow out of it when he was no longer an infant, but that never materialized.

At five years of age, their son, Jimmy, still wanted to be held and cried a lot. He still sucked his fingers, wore a diaper, and wouldn't let his mother leave his sight. Both medical and psychological specialists were consulted, but little assistance was offered other than telling Lonnie that his son had emotional problems. Desperate, Lonnie contacted me for even a glimmer of hope.

"So how bad are things?" I asked him.

Lonnie sighed, pausing for a moment, and then said, "Things aren't getting any better. We go from one doctor to the next and nothing seems to change. The medical bills are mounting." Lonnie paused, sighing deeply before continuing, "I'm thinking of putting him in a home."

"Have you discussed this with Sharon?" I asked.

"Yes, and she is dead set against it, but I see nothing else that we can do. I'm so deep in debt that I don't think we'll ever be able to afford that dream house we want. Hell, I'm going to be an old man by the time I pay these bills off, if I pay them off at all."

"Has he made any progress? Have you tried taking the diaper off?"

"He'll only poop all over the floor. Sharon still has to feed him. He won't eat alone. He'll just cry at the top of his lungs. He won't even put a cookie into his mouth unless Sharon is right there. I've never seen a kid turn away from a cookie."

"Have you been able to leave him with a sitter or a relative?"

"There's no way. He won't leave Sharon's sight. He cries and runs to her and clings to her. He even goes into the bathroom when she has to go."

"This problem is heavily rooted in karma."

"You know that I don't believe in that stuff."

"I'm aware of that, but western medicine has offered you no explanation as to why your son is like that."

"I know. And the money is really starting to add up. That stuff seems so foreign to me."

"That's because you don't understand it. Western religion keeps you focused on outward things and has drilled it into your head that there is no cause for what is going on with Jimmy."

Lonnie sighed, and then went on, "You're right, no one can explain it. I've given up on trying to find the cause for this or any rhyme or reason for such."

"I can reveal the cause to you."

Lonnie paused for longer than a moment, and then replied, "You mean that past life stuff?"

"Uh-huh."

"That stuff seems rather spooky to me."

"There's nothing spooky about it. It's just that you don't understand it."

"Let me think about it."

Lonnie returned seven weeks later, desperate for any kind of solution for what was happening with Jimmy. He showed up two hours late and was reluctant to be put under. Following some coaching that was designed to calm him down; he gave into the hypnotic process. It took some time in order to get Lonnie into a deep hypnotic state. I instructed him to go to the incarnation that was most affecting what was going on with Jimmy. I waited a little while, and then asked him, "Where are you?"

68

Lonnie paused for longer than a moment and then his facial expression changed. He said, "I'm somewhere in colonial France. I'm not exactly sure what year it is."

"It's not important. So what are you doing?"

He gasped, and then said, "Sharon is an infant that was born to a well to do family and I am a few years older. The mother is Jimmy. She was cold with me, but she completely ignored Sharon."

"Do you know why this is?"

"Because the pregnancy was unexpected and she was a society woman with an active social schedule. She saw Sharon as a nuisance that got in the way of the life that she really wanted to live."

"And how does Sharon take this?"

Lonnie gulped, pausing for a moment, and then replied, "She is acting just like Jimmy does now. She is emotional and doesn't want to let Jimmy out of her sight. Jimmy won't have anything to do with her and runs into the bedroom and slams the door whenever Sharon runs to her with outstretched arms and wants to be held."

"Go forward in time and tell me what happened," I instructed him.

Lonnie remained still for a moment and then inhaled hard, holding his breath for longer than a moment before he replied, "She died not long after. "A tear came to his eye," he went on, "She was never loved. All Jimmy had to do was show her a little attention and hold her a minute or two, but she dared not interrupt her precious social schedule." The tears flowed down his face at a good rate.

"Okay, I want you to come back down. You will remember what you saw."

Lonnie opened his eyes and looked about long before I had even counted him up. He looked at me with a penetrating gaze, projecting the image that his mind was racing with thoughts. He spoke in a single exhale, "It's the same damn thing."

"Yes it is," I replied.

"Jimmy is exactly the same as Sharon was in that lifetime in France."

"And he will continue to be so until the karma is balanced."

Lonnie looked at me with wide and curious eyes. He asked, "And how do we do that?"

"You need to give Jimmy the infantile love that Sharon didn't have in that previous incarnation."

"And how do we do that?"

"Let him sleep in bed with you. Let him coo and be an infant."

Lonnie blew a sigh of relief, and then said, "Okay, I'll try it,"

Several months later, I ran into Lonnie and asked him how Jimmy was doing. A bold smile took up a good part of his lower face. He told me that Jimmy got worse at first, constantly wanting to be held in bed, but then he changed little by little. Jimmy was soon playing by himself and giggling, something that neither Lonnie nor Sharon heard him do before, showing little care if Sharon was around or not.

Most parents think that they can grow their children like corn, that they can make them blossom into yellow corn, and they can do it all on a rigidly planned timetable. They believe that all they have to do is ride them, poke and prod them, and then apply a little guilt and presto—we have an instant business exec, attorney, or pharmacist. The fact that they did it and everyone else is doing it has them convinced that they can do it as well. But everyone else isn't doing it.

What this approach fails to realize is that there is a higher plan at work here and all this worldliness doesn't mean a thing. No one is born to merely succeed by the world's standards and become a big shot, rich, or have a name that everybody knows. To deny this higher plan is to run stark naked into a buzz saw.

Sure, it might work well with one child, but the next child may be carrying a ton of karma that must play out.

Nobody was born merely to be famous or turn a buck, but rather all of us were born to balance our karma and thus grow spiritually. In order to achieve this, each of us has been assigned a dharma, a nature that will aid us in overcoming our karma and thus grow spiritually. Dharma explains why one person was born cool and another one was born a jerk. We all know the jerk that delights in entering a room and stinking up the place with his attitude. There is no way to change such a person and it is best to apply non-resistance and avoid them.

The corporate family with the juvenile delinquent son will try to force their ways upon their son instead of trying to find the true nature of their son's behavior. Attempting to alter someone's dharma is like trying to reverse the flow of a river. Instead of confronting it head-on, they will try to hide it from others and create the delusion that their son is "normal" and walking the well-worn path that is proscribed by society.

This will fly in the face of reality if the son ends up in jail and those around the family find out about it. The family's beliefs: that the son needs religion, therapy, to play sports, different friends, different music, etc, all fly in the face of reality. The family might as well believe in the Easter Bunny or consult the Tooth Fairy to save their son. It is only by confronting the karmic forces at work here that the situation can be understood, dealt with, and then reversed.

Jerry Rubin was a radical in the 1960s and took on the establishment and its values. He considered people who wore suits, cut their hair and did as the establishment said as being plastic. Jerry wore tie died tee shirts and had long hair and a beard, neither of which were trimmed or groomed. Jerry spent his hippie career stirring up trouble and trying to be the biggest thorn in the establishment's side. This culminated in the demonstration at the 1968 Democratic Convention in Chicago where he and seven other radicals were arrested and charged with inciting a riot. The Chicago 8 were acquitted.

Jerry Rubin's dharma was to defy convention, and this didn't change after he had completed his fifth decade. Jerry, now a yuppie, clean cut and wearing a suit, just like the people that he had called plastic during his hippie days, started a networking salon for fellow yuppies. Did Jerry's dharma change? No—because Jerry was still defying convention, although in a much different way. Jerry's networking salon defied conventional networking and was on the cutting edge of the accepted way that things were done. Whether hippie or yuppie, Jerry Rubin's dharma remained the same, to defy convention.

Meditation to reveal your dharma

There is a way for you to understand the forces that are at work here and make things a whole lot easier. By knowing the dharma at work here, you will know the true reason why you, your child, or anyone else, is the way that they are. Here is what you need to do. Get into a meditative state. See a sphere of pure white light at your crown chakra. Look at a picture of yourself (your child or whoever) on the wall in front of you. See the sphere pulsate as you stare at the photo for a moment. Now mentally put a blindfold on and dig with a shovel. Your dharma will come up and reveal itself to you.

Whether you know it or not, you were destined to have the number of children that you do for karmic reasons. You also have children with certain personalities, psychological and medical problems, etc because of karmic reasons. If you have a retarded child, it is the direct result of your actions in a past life. You need to come to both understand and accept this. In this way, you can both help your retarded son and even help him overcome his retardation.

Each child will mature at different levels because of karma, as we saw in our last example with Jimmy. Most parents falsely believe that each child is not different and always compare them to other children. We aren't dealing with machines here. Holding up a ruler along side of your child, and forcing your child to live up to such rigid standards, flies in the face of reality. You need to grasp the bigger picture and understand the higher (spiritual) forces at work here.

Have you ever wondered why your parents loved or didn't love you? The fact is that it had nothing to do with your parents, but rather with your karma, and more importantly, with the love that you gave your own children in one or several of your past lives. Many people spend years in therapy trying to deal with this and struggle even for a hint of an answer as to why this occurred. What they really need to do is look at themselves and not at their parents.

Family togetherness karmically shapes you. Someone from a broken family, especially one where the parents weren't around, will have greater psychological problems then children raised in the traditional two parent family. These children will also be less balanced and less spiritual. The lack of sufficient love leads to emptiness and insanity. Though you may not be able to change what happened in your family when you were a child, you can plant new seeds with your current family.

Meditation to see your karmic family situation

There is a way for you to see the karma of the family that you were raised in and to gain understanding that you otherwise couldn't. Get into a meditative state and see a sphere of pure white light at your crown chakra. See yourself in the living room of the house or apartment that you were raised in. See the sphere at your crown chakra expand and cocoon the entire living room. Watch the parents and your siblings and the karma will be revealed to you.

Kathy was the last child of three and struggled most of her twenty-six years to maintain a lasting relationship. Love seemed to elude her, yet she clung to a glimmer of hope that Mr. Right was out there. Kathy and her older sister Grace--who was her mother's favorite--never got along despite the circumstances. Grace always got all the love and attention, including the most presents at Christmas time.

Kathy struggled to understand this her entire life, and things always got worse at Christmas time because Grace always got more than she did. She even tried to ask her mother why at one point, but just couldn't work up the nerve to do it. She was at yet another low point when she ran into me.

"My mother just bought Grace a car. She wouldn't buy me a stick," she said.

"Sorry to hear about that," I reassured her. "Was there a reason for this?"

She spoke in a sassing voice, "Because she said that her car was getting old."

"You can't change your mother. You are just going to have to accept her the way that she is."

"That's easy for you to say. She doesn't snub you while buying precious Grace everything under the sun."

"The more you resist this, and resist not getting anything while Grace gets a car, the more pain you will suffer."

"So what am I supposed to do, congratulate Grace on her new car?"

"You need to let go of it and quit trying to get love from your mother. Seek the love that you need elsewhere."

"That's what I've been doing."

"But you keep failing because of her. Don't want one red cent from her."

"That's exactly what I'm getting."

"You are expecting her to buy you something. You would even like something little that represents a token of her love. You need to let go of all of those expectations. Expect nothing from her."

"But then I'll never get anything."

"And just what have you gotten?"

She paused for longer than a moment, and then blew out a sigh. She said, "Nothing."

"It is your expectations and resistance to what *is* that is causing your problem, not your mother. Your mother can only affect you if you let her."

"That's a bunch of malarkey."

"Think about it. You are clinging to your mother giving you something."

"Well she bought Grace a damn car."

"And you are clinging to the notion that she is going to buy you something next. You need to let go of this and move on."

"But she bought Grace a car."

"And you are clinging to it. It isn't whether or not she buys Grace a car, but how *you* react to it."

Kathy sighed, and then replied, "Okay, I'll try to expect nothing from my mom."

"It will work. I promise."

Kathy struggled with this for several months, but gradually let go of her expectations of getting anything from her mother. She found a new guy nine weeks later, one who buys her things.

INTIMACY

Sex is a commodity that is bought and sold. It is packaged and displayed on TV shows and in the movies. On the screen, you see beautiful and buff women, who in real life workout for several hours each day to maintain those flat stomachs. They parade around in their underwear just to draw in your sexual curiosity. The men are equally as muscular, having to workout even longer than the women do. These images leave us with a false sense of intimacy, leading us to believe that it's all about looks and going to bed.

If you want a soul mate, then you're going to have to learn to be intimate. Many people falsely believe that intimacy involves only sex. Communication, caressing, fondling, foreplay, and kissing are only some of the qualities involved. Your soul mate will open up all these levels for you, and then take them to new and exciting heights. But you have to be ready for it.

Much of intimacy involves communication, but this isn't limited to mere verbal statements. We can speak thousands of words with a smile, a touch, or by giving our soul mate a present. On a more metaphysical level, we communicate with our thoughts. If you think only of your soul mate, then your soul mate will think about you. Add a positive emotion or love behind the thought and your soul mate will get the message. Take it one step further and add the image of yourself smiling. You are sure to bring a smile to your soul mate's face.

For intimacy to work with your soul mate, it has to start early in the relationship. Gatherings of all sorts are prime dating ground. Too many people move way too fast toward the bedroom. One night stands, and other short-term affairs, are common under such circumstances. Intimacy needs time, not only to grow, but to blossom. Many people never experience it in its fullness, but this doesn't have to be.

Many people make the mistake of going to the movies on their first few dates. It's better to go to places that lead to conversation, places that require you to slow down and get to know the person you are with. Leave your cell phone at home. You could even go for walks or just sit on a park bench. You should avoid, at least for the first several weeks, noisy bars and restaurants and any other such environments.

Sex can be a fun part of dating, but you have to be careful in this age of AIDS. Many people who fall head over heels in love lose all sense of precaution, becoming absorbed in the giddy feeling of love. Even though someone is your soul mate, and you have been with her through several life times, you shouldn't jump in bed without a condom on.

Just because you're in love, doesn't mean that sex is some sort of casual event. Sex is to be taken seriously and as part of the growth process. Most couples jump into bed way too early in the relationship, sometimes on the first date. Most people believe, and do so rather falsely, that sex will help them get to know their partner. Nothing magical is going to happen during intercourse other than orgasm.

Metaphysical warning of sexual partners to be avoided

There are certain people that we should stay away from, but they aren't always wearing signs around their necks to tell us this. Most people think they can pick out who has STDs and who doesn't or that only a certain kind of people get them. There is something you can do to warn yourself and pick these people out, something that could end up saving you much grief or even from a premature death.

There is a way to probe your perspective partner with your higher mind and have it warn you if you should stay away from him. This technique should not be undertaken lightly, or with any other purpose in mind than the one that I intend.

Do the chakra balancing and protection and then breathe in a 2/4 rhythm. You need to do this longer than you usually do and bring on a deep, meditative state. I want you to see a sphere of pure white light coming out of your third eye chakra. See it going about five feet from you and hovering there. The sphere is glistening with pure white light.

I now want you to select an image or thought form for your higher self to send to you. Now focus on the sphere, saying to it out loud:

I give you the mission of warning me of any sex partners that I should stay away from. At the moment I meet someone that I should stay away from, you will send the image of an AIDS poster (or whatever you want) *into my conscious mind.*

Now mentally will it to go and see it going away from you. Know that though it is no longer visible, it is still close to you.

You are going to have to keep the sphere charged with energy if you want it to keep working for you. Once a week, mentally summon it and see it appear in front of you. Breathe in the 2/4 rhythm and get into a relaxed state. Send golf ball sized spheres from your third eye into the sphere, seeing it get both whiter and brighter. Once again tell it what you want it to do and then send it on its way.

Kate W. met a man at a New Age gathering and felt certain that he was her soul mate. It wasn't long after she was dating, that a funny rash broke out on her vagina, one that became worse as the days progressed. She waited as long as she could, but she couldn't put off seeing a doctor any longer. Her worst fears were realized; she had gonorrhea.

Kate confronted Dave and to her surprise discovered that he had already known that he had it and was undergoing treatment. Kate, who moved out of Dave's house almost immediately, lost all faith in soul mates and spirituality. She went through medical treatment alone and bitter. It wasn't far into her treatment that she ran into me.

"Your stupid soul mate theories jumped up and bit me in the ass," she snapped.

"I'm sorry that you got sick, but New Age theories had nothing to do with it," I said.

"*Bull*," she snapped, "I thought I was in this perfect love relationship that went back several life times."

"That doesn't mean you can throw caution to the wind. Just because someone is your soul mate it doesn't make them perfect," I said.

"And I suppose that I had some sort of karmic predisposition to come down with this," she said.

"Maybe you did," I said.

"And what was this supposed to teach me?" She sassed.

"Any number of things," I said.

"Like what?" She crossed her arms and pouted.

"We could explore that if you want to," I said.

"Don't waste your breath," she said.

"Have you ever fallen in love like this before?" I asked.

"You mean have I ever gotten clap before? I'm not some kind of slut who gets clap on an annual basis," she huffed.

"That's not what I meant," I said.

"But that's what you said," she said.

"That's not what I said. I didn't mean the gonorrhea. I meant have you ever been blinded by love before?" I asked.

"What's it to ya?" She spat out.

"Maybe there's a lesson that you have to learn," I said.

She stared at me for a prolonged moment and then lit a cigarette. She took a big puff and then blew out her smoke in a sigh, making sure that it drifted up in my face. She waited a moment, and then said, "It happened once before, but I never got VD from it."

"That's a lesson that you need to learn. This is why it keeps coming up again and again," I said.

"A lot of good it does me now." She took another puff and made sure the smoke drifted up in my face once again.

80

"It will if you learn the lesson that you need to learn," I said.

"I don't think I'm likely to forget it," she said.

"Wisdom destroys karma. If you've learned your lesson then there's no need to repeat the experience. Do you want me to regress you so you can know the origin of love blinding you?" I asked.

"I'd rather not know," she sighed boldly, and then said, "but I have to know. Okay, let's do it."

It took Kate sometime to calm down and it required a little extra time to put her under hypnosis. I instructed Kate to go back to the lifetime that was the source of her problems. I asked her, "So where are you?"

Kate didn't respond for a prolonged moment, and then said, "I'm in England during the Middle Ages."

"And what are you doing?" I asked.

"I'm working on a farm that is on the outskirts of a large city," she said.

"Ask your higher mind what city it is," I asked.

Kate's facial expression changed, and then she said following a long pause, "It's Blackpool."

"And what are you doing?" I asked.

"I'm feeding hay to a group of sheep that I'm in charge of. Several other young women are working with me. A mean man is in charge. He paces around with a mean look on his face. He'll yell at me or even beat me if I stop working for even a moment," she said.

"Are you married? Is there someone there that you're in love with?" I asked.

"I'm not married, but I have a lover. He's one of the sheep herders," she said.

"So what's his name? Is it someone that you know now?" I asked.

"It's someone that I dated back in school. He's the first boy I went all the way with," she said.

"Were you blinded by being in love with him?" I asked.

"Oh God, yes. After I made love with him the first time, I followed him around for two weeks," she said.

"And did anything bad happen?" I asked.

"We did it at a party after a football game. The whole school knew about it. I couldn't stand to go to school, but if I didn't, my parents would know that something was wrong," she said.

"Did they find out?" I asked.

"No, but going to school was hell. People called me a slut and some jerk painted the word *whore* on my locker," she said.

"Getting back to England. What was the man's name while you lived in England?" I asked.

"William," she said.

"And what's he doing right now?" I asked.

"He's not there. He must be out tending the flocks," she said.

"I want you to go forward to the time where he blinded you with his love and got you into trouble," I instructed.

The expression on Kate's face changed and then it became blank. She paused, and then said; "It was several days later. I was working in the barn when William grabbed me and dragged me into the loft. He laid me down and began kissing me. Joy overtook me and I felt happier than I had ever felt in my life. The feeling built and built and then—" Her voice choked off. Her lips quivered and a snarl appeared on her forehead.

"So what happened?" I asked.

"William flailed with pain and rolled off me. As I looked up, the boss was standing over me with a leather strap. The joy that I had felt just a moment ago turned into sheer terror. The boss sucked in his lips and then brought the strap down on me. As soon as I felt the pain, I passed out," she said.

"So what happened?" I inquired.

"He beat me several times. My back was a bloody mess. I didn't get out of bed for a week and had to be nursed back to health by several of my co-workers. As soon as I was well, I was driven off into the city. I never found true love again," she said.

"And what happened to William?" I asked.

"I don't know. I never saw him again. I imagine they beat him and drove him off as well," she said.

I brought Kate back into consciousness. She cried for some time and then wanted to talk about what had happened. She had come face to face with something that had been plaguing her since she had begun dating, something that was deeply karmic in nature. The pattern would've continued to repeat had she not learned the lesson.

Kate's medical treatment was successful, but the emotional pain took much longer to heal. She didn't date again for over a year, breaking up with her new man before the relationship became intimate. She didn't have sex for almost another six months and even then the emotional pain lingered.

Intimacy, and especially sex, involves touch. This doesn't have to involve fondling, but in most cases it does. Touch can range anywhere from resting your hand on your partner to heavy petting. The important thing to remember is not to rush into foreplay. Express your love and your caring with your touch and not just your horniness. Holding hands will do in most cases.

Your touch should lead you into new levels of physical responsiveness. Too many people direct this energy into horniness, which usually short circuits love. If you must rush straight into sexual arousal, try to mix in your tenderness with it. In this way, you're not merely acting out of carnal lust.

Sex, which is spiritual, is much more than a release or a carnal act. The problem is that because we've all had a guilt trip laid on us about how dirty or sinful it is that we shut out its spiritual aspects. You've been told to be prudent, repress your innate desires, and deny your own feelings. The churches then lay a whole new layer of guilt on you. What you learn is not the spirituality of sex or the proper way to approach it, but how to repress it.

When you eat your forbidden fruit, a new consciousness opens up to you. This is the very consciousness that society doesn't want you to know about. Society sets up taboos and rules for proper conduct. Thus, it's okay to buy porn as long as it's delivered in a brown box by UPS. It is to be kept out of stores, off shelves, and out of sight. Strip bars are confined to a red light district and the TV networks are tightly regulated. The last thing anyone wants is for naked hippies to be doing it out in the open for everyone to see. Marriage is tightly defined with group marriage being taboo, though gay marriage is gaining acceptance all the time.

Eating of the forbidden fruit can be a spiritual experience. If it is done right, the new knowledge that you gain can lead to oneness with the Self. The ego no longer identifies with what society wants it to do, but rather with a whole new level that has opened up to it.

When the hippies broke through the taboo that said sex should be only done in the bedroom with the lights out, a revolution ensued. The naked body was beautiful, marriage was no longer necessary, and new ways of being emerged. Great experimentation redefined traditional roles. Group marriage, wife swapping, shacking up, and multiple partners defined the sixties. And like all forbidden fruit, once it has been eaten, there is no going back.

Sexual aliveness

You don't need drugs to experience the fullness of sex, or even booze for that matter. In our disposable society, everything has to be quick, and the pharmaceutical behemoths have a pill for every problem. It's all a matter of taking the right dope—the little blue pills that make you stiff. We have become so brainwashed by these pills that we believe there is no other way to handle this.

There is a better way, an ancient way that the Chinese have been using for thousands of years. Chi is energy that can be used to heal you or even defend you. It has been used to prolong life, cure bad habits, and energize the body. You can also use it for sexual aliveness.

Breathe in a simple rhythm, allowing your stomach to go out as you inhale and come in as you exhale. After you have done this for several minutes, see your breath going to an area several inches below your belly button. Visualize your breath going there. Mentally direct it there with your will.

Now, mentally direct the chi into your genitals. You may feel a warming sensation there, your genitals may tingle, and you could even become turned on. Let it build. It is best to do this with your partner right before you have intercourse.

You can build up to some really powerful orgasms. It has been said that with repeated and daily practice, one can even increase the size of one's penis.

Hank J. was a blue-collar guy whose life was going pretty much as expected when he found his soul mate. But with his good luck came a stroke of bad luck—he couldn't get his penis to function properly. It seemed like he hit a brick wall the moment he met his soul mate, as though an evil witch had put a curse on him in one of his past lives.

Hank tried several things before going to the doctor. When he took Viagra, his heart raced out of control and he had to be rushed to the emergency room. It was several weeks later that he ran into me, certain that some sort of cosmic force was out to get him.

"Is there some sort of incense that I can burn to Buddha or something?" He asked.

"How did the chi work?" I asked him.

"It didn't. Nothing worked. I've always been ready when the woman is, but ever since I met Tammy, I haven't gotten it up once," he said.

"There has to be something in one of your past lives that's blocking you from experiencing the fullness of your love with Tammy," I said.

"Will you regress me?" He looked at me with wide eyes.

"Sure," I said.

I hypnotized Hank and had him in a deep trance within fifteen minutes. I led him back to the past life that was the origin of his problem. When his facial expression changed, I asked, "Where are you?"

"I don't know. There's a lot of activity here," he said.

"Well ask--" I began.

"That's the Coliseum. I'm in Rome," he interrupted.

"Do you know what year it is?" I probed.

He paused for longer than a moment, and then said, "Ten seventy-three."

"So where are you?" I asked.

"I just stepped into the back door of a church." He paused for a moment, and then gasped, "Oh my God."

"What is it?" I asked.

"I'm a priest," he said.

"What are you doing?" I questioned.

"I'm there on orders from the Vatican. I'm yelling at the priests that are there," he said.

"Why are you doing this?" I asked.

"The Vatican wants priests to be celibate. Most of the priests have wives." He choked and then began to cry, "I am forbidding them from ever having sex again. I have to tear some of the women from them. They are to be sold into slavery." He sobbed for longer than a moment.

"So what's going on now?" I asked.

"One woman in particular is putting up a fight. She is several months pregnant. *Oh my God, it's Tammy.* I'm ordering the guards to use greater force. They're beating her." His voice broke, "She's beat about the face and they're dragging her off."

"It's okay. I want you to return to consciousness. I'm

going to bring you back on 5-4-3-2-1. Open your eyes. You will remember everything that happened under hypnosis," I said.

Hank burst into tears, and then said, "I'm sorry."

"You've paid for what you have done. You've balanced your karma," I said.

"That doesn't make me feel any better," he said.

"It will. Give it a few days," I instructed.

Several days after I regressed Hank, he achieved an erection.

MONEY

One of the central issues in any relationship is money, and it's not about getting all that you can or handing your loved one everything. Many poor people have healthy relationships, but they make intelligent decisions about spending what they have. Unless you make such decisions as a couple, money can quickly drive soul mates apart, or even become the only issue in a relationship, which is much more than sitting around and paying bills.

Many couples merge their money into one joint account, though each of them usually has some cash of their own tucked away or the wife has a "secret" credit card. From a metaphysical standpoint, the two beings and consciousnesses are becoming one. Neither partner holds any money back, nor do they work alone at managing the account.

This was the structure of the parents of most baby boomers, one account per family. Mom only had the money that dad put into the checking account. All of the expenses came from that one account, which required that the partners communicate with each other so they knew just what the current balance was.

The age of divorce changed all of this and most women these days have some money of their own, usually coming from employment if only part-time. Many people say that having separate accounts is preplanning for a break up. Remember that your mind hears every word that you speak or think, and it reacts to your intentions. The two of you need to have clear intentions about the account.

A counter argument says that having some money of your own gives you freedom. This could strengthen a relationship, or perhaps hurt it, by making the weaker partner independent of the chief breadwinner. This is far more common in relationships where both partners hold jobs.

This brings us to the whole notion of secret money. Should you hide money from your partner? And if you do, aren't you already cheating in your mind? Remember that everything that occurs in reality takes place first in the mind. Is there a difference between hiding money and hiding a lover?

I'm not going to tell you "the right way" to handle the money in your relationship, or provide you with rigid answers that you must goose step to. What works for one couple is utter folly to another couple. What is more important is that the two of you plan and agree on how to handle the money.

The bank in your mind

Many people come to me and ask me the metaphysical "secret" of how to make vast amounts of money, which assumes that money is separate from you and that duality is the basis of reality. And I always tell them that you have to eliminate your separateness from money long before you'll ever have it in the bank. And then I explain the truth about wealth to them, which is actually the same as poverty.

Wealth and poverty are two *names* for the same thing. By focusing only on these names and forms, you are missing the true nature of money. You already have money, but your delusions, names, and forms have locked you in a prison that has kept you out of its flow. I am going to show you how to remove these delusions and remove what separates you from money.

Doubling the amount of money that you make isn't going to make your life twice as good, it may very well make it worse. Wealth is a state of mind and the material possessions are only a *symbol* of the wealth consciousness that you have. Someone with a Rolls Royce may not be wealthy at all. The car, and everything else, can be hawked to high heaven. The *symbols* of wealth aren't wealth themselves and can be delusions.

Here is the Zen meditation that will release your delusions of separation and cause money to flow to you. First, get into a meditative state. See a sphere of pure white light at your crown chakra. Now see an umbrella of white light four inches above the sphere. See the sphere pulsate and chant *All is one.* Let the umbrella fade away, visualizing only the sphere of pure white light at your crown chakra. Do this once a day, twice if possible, for at least five minutes.

Another way to get more money is to put more value on what you do to obtain your money. Too many of us discount the work that we do as average or tell ourselves that anybody can do it. I don't mean that you should become arrogant or boastful, but that you should see your work as having more value in your mind. You will likely get a raise for doing so.

A third way to have more money is to see the money that you do have as abundance. If you believe that what you have is lack, then you will always be lacking. The more you think that you don't have money for this or you don't have money for that or that you can't pay your bills, the less money you will have in the future for these things.

A final way to have more money is to stop thinking about the money that you spend as being gone. Instead see that money returning to you threefold, see it flowing all around you. Every time you pull a bill or credit card out of your wallet, say to those bills, in your private speech, *you will return to me.* Know in your heart that it will come back to you. Fully believe it. You will be surprised how that money returns to you.

Diane D. had nine credit cards that were each maxed out, several of them in collection, one creditor threatening to sue. She had to file bankruptcy, but the very thought of it terrified her to the bones. Whatever she did, money seemed to fly away from her. She asked me if there was anything she could do to turn things around.

"What are your thoughts concerning money?" I asked her.

"What do you mean?" She looked at me with a perplexed look on her face.

"How do you view money in your mind?" I asked her.

"I never have enough of it," she said.

"What is the first thought that comes into your mind when you get a bill?" I asked.

"*Oh my God,*" she said.

"That's a good part of your problem. You see money as something that's flowing away from you," I said.

"So what am I supposed to do, hang onto it?" she said.

"That would be just as bad. To hoard something is to believe in scarcity and lack. The tighter you hold onto it, the less money there will be in your life," I said.

"I already tried spending it like water, but that didn't work," she said.

"But you viewed money as flying away from you and you spent it in a reckless manner, which only made it fly away all the quicker," I said.

"Do you have some magic seeds that will sprout trees that grow tens and twenties?" She asked in a playful tone.

"I wish I did," I returned the smile, "but you can take a different approach to money. The first thing you need to do is to think about money in a whole new way. Don't see it as something that is flowing away from you," I said. I then explained to her how to see money returning to her.

"That might work after I file bankruptcy." She sighed, "But even that isn't going to pay off all these credit cards that have sky high interest rates," she said.

"What do those credit cards symbolize for you? How do you feel when you use them?" I inquired.

Her face lit up, and she smiled when she said, "I feel good when I spend money. I like the feeling of being in the mall and having the power to buy whatever I want."

"But you're going into debt to do it. Like most people in your situation, you're confusing debt with an asset. Getting a credit card with a two thousand dollar limit is not the same as getting a two thousand dollar raise," I said.

"Do they play subliminal messages under the music at the malls?" She grinned.

"Supposedly. But you still have the free will to act," I said.

"When I'm at the mall, I can't resist the urge to spend," she said.

"It's easy to blame it on subliminal messages," I said.

"But I don't feel that way at McDonald's," she said.

"What do they have at the mall that makes you feel so good about buying?" I asked.

"The subliminal messages." She smiled.

"What is the bulk of the charges on your credit card?" I asked.

She had to think for a moment, and then replied," Mostly clothing for myself."

"And how does having new clothes make you feel?" I asked.

She grinned and then replied, "How do you think they make me feel?"

"I don't know. Describe it for me," I said.

"I feel like the women in all the magazines. I feel glamorous and attractive," she said.

"You can't let giddy school girl feelings dominate your spending," I said.

"It's hard to avoid. I don't think I can stay away from the mall," she said.

"But that doesn't mean that you have to buy everything. You can't continue to allow money to flow away from you like that," I said.

"I feel so good wearing new clothes and new shoes," she said.

"What are you going to do when they shut the credit cards off?" I asked.

Diane's grin left her immediately and a perplexed look dominated her face. She said, "I don't know."

"You have to begin seeing money flowing to you," I said.

"Will that bail me out of these credit card debts?" She asked.

"I doubt it. That die has already been cast. Unless you begin to see money flowing to you, things can only become worse," I said.

"Damn," she replied.

I asked Diane if she would like to undergo regression and see if there were any past lives that were affecting her current situation with money. To my surprise, she agreed right away with a smile on her face. I put her under not long afterwards and instructed her to go to the incarnation that was most plaguing her. I asked her, "Where are you?"

"It looks like some sort of medieval city. The streets are narrow and dirty. Garbage is everywhere. People of means ride their horses and carriages without care about those of us who are poor. If they trampled us to death, our bodies would lay there and rot. No one would care," she replied.

"So you are poor?"

"Yes. Very poor. I am dressed in rags and live off the apple cores and trash that those who ride the horses throw away. My teeth are rotted and I am in bad shape health wise."

"And how old are you?"

"Seventeen."

"Do you have any family?"

"Yes, but they have all scattered. My father was killed in an accident and we lost everything. We had to live on the street eventually, and my mom went insane. Me and my sister and brother scattered, each going our separate ways. I haven't seen either of them since."

"Are you deep in debt to someone?"

"No, I want to have good clothes and dress like the women in the carriages who spit on me."

"Do you know any of these women?"

"No. I wish I did. I feel dirty and lower than a dog. I wouldn't dare look one of these women in the eye let alone speak to one of them."

"How do you feel when you see what they are wearing?"

Her face lit up and she smiled from ear to ear. She replied, "I would feel like a princess on the night of the ball. I would feel like I was somebody and that I belonged in the world and a place that was all mine."

"Do you fantasize about having clothes like that?"

The smile remained on her face as she replied, "Oh God, yes. Every time there's enough food in my belly to keep hunger at bay for a little while."

"Is there any way for you to get any clothes?"

"No. Once you are on the streets like that they leave you for dead."

"So what happened?"

"I found some old curtains in a garbage can one time. I had so many ideas in my head I couldn't think straight. I thought that I could fashion them into one of the outfits I saw the women in the carriages wear, but in the end all I managed to create was a mess."

"What did you do?"

"I cried for days. I even tried to throw myself under a carriage, but some man shoved me away and yelled at me."

"Did you ever get any clothes in that incarnation?"

Her facial expression turned somber. She gasped, and then said, "No, I died a few years later of an infection."

I brought Diane back into consciousness and she quickly realized why she bought so many clothes and why she felt the way she did about them. Over the course of the next few weeks, her spending habits pulled back from being obsessive.

One of the biggest problems people have concerning money is expectations. As soon as you're paired up, society has certain expectations for how you are to live.

Though it might be all right for a single man to live in some run-down basement apartment, a couple is expected to have their own house (or at least a nice apartment).

Comparisons and judgments poke and prod people into trying to live beyond their means.

TV commercials hold up examples of what society expects of you. Not only are you supposed live the life of suburbia, but you are supposed to live as they proscribe. You are to have no long hair, follow mainstream religions, listen to "normal" music, etc. Just like in the TV commercials.

The problem is that people spend more money trying to live up to these expectations than they make, leaving them with a life that centers on sitting around and paying bills. This can destroy even the most stable of relationships. People end up giving their lives over to money and material objects because they feel societal pressures telling them that this is what they're supposed to have.

Your partner also has financial expectations, which the two of you need to discuss. You must be sure that your partner's expectations are in line with the family budget; otherwise, you will end up in a downward spiral where money is flowing away from you. You should talk about money with your partner and let them know how much you are making so that spending doesn't fly out of control.

You should sit down and plan as a couple, including just how much debt you are willing to take on. It's important that the two of you think alike concerning money. Plan to have money flowing to you, and structure your thoughts concerning money accordingly. It is important that you touch base on money at least once a month, just to be sure that you're both going in the same direction.

Another source of financial pressure is your in-laws. Many fine marriages have disintegrated due to pressures from the in-laws as regards to what you are supposed to have and where you are supposed to live. Relatives always compare you to similar others—check out where Betty is living, Ralph just got a promotion and a new car, etc. In the worst cases, there is nagging and put-downs. You are deemed somehow inferior or you're not an adequate father because an adequate father buys this, that, and everything for his family.

Money merger

Like two corporations that are being thrust together, a marriage thrusts two different financial situations together. This can be the merger of good with good or the merger of good with bad. If one partner is someone who has a juicy savings account and the other partner has four credit cards, all of which are close to being maxed out, then some important decisions are going to have to be made.

The two partners need to sit facing each other. You might want to turn the lights out and light a candle. Join hands, gaze into each other's eyes, and take a few moments to relax. See your third eyes opening and then see a white beam of light connecting them. Now see money flowing between the two of you. The flowing proceeds at a slow pace, yet the exchange of money is consistent. See that equal amounts of money are both coming and going from each partner.

Now, see a sphere of white light coming out of your crown chakra. You can signal to your partner when it is time to do this by arranging some sort of hand signal beforehand. See droplets of white light raining down on you, raining at a steady rate from your sphere. See your rain and your partner's rain mixing to such a point that you can no longer tell which sphere is sending rain down upon you.

Now, see the flow of money between your third eyes increasing, and only a little at a time. See it building at a steady rate, becoming rather fast. At the same time, see the rain pouring down on you.

With a hand signal, instruct your partner to stop. See the sphere going back into your crown chakra and see your third eye closing. It is best to either hug or kiss at this point.

Karen B. thought that her relationship with Chuck was over when she got an unexpected lawsuit in the mail. She had a credit card about eleven years ago that she didn't pay. When the bank quit calling her, she thought the bad mark on her credit report would remain for the next seven years and that would be the end of it.

She hired a lawyer, but it didn't do her any good. The debt was good for fifteen years, and she had no other choice but to pay it. Though the lawyer managed to get the interest rate reduced, he couldn't stop the garnishment.

Karen almost lost her job, and just to make matters worse, her company added another 12% garnishment fee on top of what the court was taking out of her check. She had to get someone to take over the payments on her car before the bank repossessed it. With both her checking and savings accounts completely garnished, she was reduced to cashing what remained of her paycheck at a payday loan place.

Karen became depressed and began drinking heavily. Her friends had to talk Chuck into staying with her, both times. The toll became great on Karen, and became even greater when she had to move out of her apartment and move back home with her mother. It wasn't long after her return home that I ran into her.

"Can you tell if somebody put a hex on me?" Karen asked.

"Somebody might have put a hex on you, but it's more than likely something from one of your past lives," I said.

"This guy is so sleazy and arrogant. He takes such delight in throwing it in my face and screwing everybody over that he comes in contact with," she said.

"Perhaps you were that way in one of your past lives," I said.

"There's no way in hell that I was ever like that," she said.

"But it's possible that you were. Many people are vastly different now from what they were in another incarnation. In many cases, they are the opposite of what they were in the previous incarnation. In this way, they workout their karma," I said.

"Even if I was like that, that still doesn't explain why this happened now. Why didn't it happen when I had the credit card?" She asked.

"Maybe it has to do with timing. Or maybe it has to do with your thinking that you've gotten away with something," I said.

"I didn't think it was legal for them to sell these old loans to sleazebags like him," she said.

"Maybe you were the sleazebag in a past life," I suggested.

Karen sighed, and then asked, "Even if I did do something in a past life, what can I do now to get out of this mess?"

"Understanding the karma involved might lessen the blow or even get rid of the debt altogether," I said.

"I'm not real sure about this. I've never done it before," she said.

"Have you discovered one of your past lives in another way or perhaps even in a dream?" I asked.

"I kind of have these feelings, but I really haven't seen any scenes." She wrung her hands.

"I think this is something you need to explore," I suggested.

"Am I going to freak out or have nightmares?" She wrung her hands.

"Maybe in extreme cases, but I've never heard of anyone having a nightmare as the result of being regressed," I stated.

"I'm still not sure about this. I mean, once I see it, that door will be open," she said.

"It's not as bad as you think. You already know that you've lived before. It's just like watching a television program," I said.

"If it'll get rid of this mess, then I'll do it, but I really don't want to," she said.

"It'll be all right," I reassured her.

I regressed Karen and brought her back to the lifetime where the debt had occurred. Despite her reservations, she went under fast. I instructed her to go to the day that the debt occurred. I asked her, "So where are you?"

"I'm in Alexandria during the height of the Egyptian Empire," she said.

"Describe for me what you're doing," I instructed.

"I'm a man—I'm a big muscular man," she said.

"So what are you doing?" I asked.

"I'm in charge of a bunch of other men. One of them has a bunch of scrolls with the names of people who owe taxes. The other men are soldiers. They have swords and spears," she said.

"So what are you doing?" I asked.

"I'm searching the market for a man that I've been looking for for sometime. Suddenly, there is a commotion at a pottery booth in front of me. *There he is.* I yell to the soldiers to get him. They run around me and catch up with him. They drag him back to me. The man is squirming and pleading. I motion with my head for him to get it in the ribs. One of the soldiers gives him the butt end of a spear in the ribs. The man falls to the ground in pain," she said.

"And what about the debt?" I asked.

"The man with the scroll reads off what he owes. The man who owes the taxes is pleading for mercy. He says that we already took his house, all his possessions, and his animals. He said that he thought that he had paid the debt. I order the soldiers to cart him off to prison. The man is begging and crying, but I insist that he pay his taxes," she said.

"Okay, I want you to return to consciousness. You're coming back up and when we get to one, you will open your eyes. 5-4-3-2-1," I said.

Karen opened her eyes and then looked around the room for several moments before gazing at me.

"So what are you feeling?" I asked her.

"I'm not sure," she said.

"So how do you feel about the debt?" I asked.

"I'm not angry about it any more. I understand where it came from and why. I no longer see it as some random event that just fell out of the sky," she said.

"That's good," I said.

"Will the debt go away now?" She asked.

"Maybe, maybe not. But you're now better able to handle it," I said.

The garnishment of Karen's paycheck continued. She learned to live with what she had left of her paycheck and eventually moved out of her mother's house.

OPEN YOUR HEART

What is in your heart is what is in your life. If your heart is closed to love, then you will live such a life. Many of us shut out the very love that we want by our hardened attitudes and judgments of others. These attitudes take root in the mind, and then on the spiritual level. Your attitudes and thoughts form the reality that you live, thus you can change the reality that you are now living by changing your thoughts and attitudes.

Your heart chakra is the gateway to true and divine love, a gateway that most people have either partially or totally shut out. Thus most people's experience of love is very limited, and it usually gravitates around the lower animal aspects of love. They base love on looks, social status, and other outward things. It is the rare person who bases their love on higher, spiritual aspects.

In order to open your heart, you have to first know what love is. You have to give up your false notions of love if you are to truly experience it. Begin by treating everyone that you encounter with love, respond out of love, and think only loving thoughts. I know this sounds easy, but it's really a tall order. We want to be right, to have the upper hand, or to throw it in somebody's face. All of these attitudes are infantile and egotistical. Try another approach. Try love.

You must accept people, especially your partner, just the way that they are. This is also a tall order, but a worthwhile one to accomplish. Once you accept people just as they are, you will find no reason to blame or judge. With this acceptance, comes the acceptance of your partner's limitations and humanness. Don't expect them to give more love than they are capable of. Accept the love that they do give you as abundance, and treat it as such.

Open your heart chakra

This exercise will open your heart chakra and may bring

emotions to life in you that you may feel uncomfortable with. You may feel some tightness in your chest, but there is no need to worry. This is your heart chakra opening, which may also bring emotions to the surface.

The first thing you want to do is make sure you're alone and that no one will disturb you. Take a few minutes to breathe in the 2/4 rhythm and get into a meditative state. Make sure you feel your body relax and that there is a light feeling about you. See a sphere of pure white light at your crown chakra, taking several moments to see it pulsate. Now see a line of white light going down from this sphere to your heart chakra.

Now visualize a red sphere coming out of your heart and remaining there, seeing the white line and sphere at your crown chakra fade. See it becoming redder and sparkling with life. You may feel tightness in your chest or your emotions welling up, but this is okay. Now I want you to focus on your breathing. Imagine each inhalation going to your heart, seeing it as pure white light.

You can merely hold this for a few minutes and then stop or you can take it to the next level. You can ask your heart questions if you want, making sure to keep the above visualization and meditation going. You can ask it if you are ready for a soul mate or what you need to do in order to experience love more fully. Or you can ask it any similar question. It will usually respond with a feeling, which you may not understand at first. Don't be afraid to ask again. If you feel positive and warm, then you know that the answer is yes.

Karla D. was fast approaching thirty and grew increasingly frustrated at her mother's nagging that she was an old maid. She just couldn't find the right man. None of her past relationships came close to marriage, and none of those men so much as hinted at popping the question. Though she was successful in her chosen career and had a nice apartment, her mother's nagging bothered her. She felt incomplete, as though she had only managed to get two out of three and was still lacking. It was after one of her mother's nags that she ran into me.

"So what's the big deal about turning thirty?" I asked her.

"You wouldn't understand. It's different for a woman," she said.

"There's an ocean of single women who are thirty and beyond," I said.

"But most of them have married by this point," she said.

"There are plenty of single women that age working for the top corporations. I would hardly say that *most* women that age were married," I said.

"Everybody that I know is married. People are talking about me," she said.

"Who?" I asked.

"Everybody," she spoke with her hands. "I can't even find a guy to stay with me for longer than six months."

"Your expectations are in conflict with reality," I said.

"So how do I make reality conform to my expectations?" She asked with a determined look on her face.

"You can't. But you can change your expectations," I said.

"What about my mom?" She asked.

"You can't change her. She's going to have to change on her own. But you can change the way in which you deal with her," I said.

"So what am I supposed to do, become a guru?" She asked.

"All you need to do is change the way that you view things. Instead of viewing your mother as a nag who's pressuring you about getting married, see her as she is, warts and all," I said.

"That's easy for you to say. You've never met my mother. Deal with her for five minutes and you'll know what I'm talking about," she said.

"We all have difficult people that we have to deal with and we all have people that we don't get alone with. The way to handle it is to accept them the way that they are without judgment or blame," I said.

"That's not going to work if my mother keeps nagging me," she said.

"It won't change your mother, but it will change the way that you deal with your mother and the way that you handle her nagging," I said.

Karla sighed, and then said, "Okay, I'll try it. But is it going to help me find a guy that will stay with me longer than a few months?" She asked.

"For that, I'm going to have to regress you," I said.

"Anything to get out of this mess," she said.

I regressed Karla and instructed her to go back to the lifetime where her problems with finding a lasting relationship began. I asked her, "So where are you?"

"I'm not sure. Somewhere in the middle of a vast desert," she said.

"What are you doing?" I asked.

"I'm a man and I'm in charge of the camels. I'm part of a large caravan that's traveling across the desert. There are several tents set up and one of them is quite large. The man in that tent is a rich man and all of this is for him," she said.

"So what are you doing now?" I asked.

"One of the camels is throwing a fit. It's jumping about and spitting. I got a rope around its neck, but I still can't get it to calm down," she said.

"So what does the camel have to do with you not being able to obtain a lasting love relationship?" I asked.

"Another man, who is my friend, is helping me tie it down. When we have the camel secure, he smiles at me and asks, 'How long this time?' He is referring to the woman I abandoned in the last town that we were in. I smiled at him and said, 'three weeks,' " she said.

"Were you serious with this woman?" I probed.

"I'm never serious with any of them, but I tell them I am. I know that I'm going to ride out with the next caravan that crosses the desert. I have to, it's my job," she said.

"And what about the woman you left behind? How is she reacting?" I asked.

"She's shocked. She thought we were getting serious, but I never had any intention of such," she said.

"And what about her feelings? Did you care that you might be hurting her?" I asked.

"I pretended to and at times I really did care, but I knew I wouldn't be staying long. My work keeps me on the move," she said.

"Okay, I want you to return to consciousness. You're slowly coming back up and on the count of 5 you will be wide-awake. 1-2-3-4-5," I said.

Karla smiled from ear to ear as soon as she opened her eyes.

"What are you smiling about?" I asked.

"Because I discovered a secret. It's like knowing something that you weren't supposed to know," she said.

"So what do you know?" I asked.

"Why my life is the way that it is. And I always thought it was fate that some people live better than others," she said.

"It's not fate, it's karma. You do it to yourself," I said.

Several months later, Karla found a new boyfriend and her life has never been the same.

We choose to close our hearts in many ways and often we aren't aware that we are doing so. We choose to be mean or take revenge on people, thinking that we are so right about what we're doing. By doing this, we fail to understand the true nature of karma. The meanness will return to you, often many times stronger than you sent it out.

Jesus treated everyone that he came in contact with out of love, even people that were doing wrong. In one story, a crowd of people were about to stone a prostitute to death when Jesus walked up. He said that whoever didn't sin should be the one to cast the first stone. He didn't judge the crowd or condemn what they were doing, but responded out of pure love. He could've said 'you're a drunkard,' 'you steal,' or 'you sleep with loose women,' but he didn't. This is how open your heart has to be. Even if you see someone doing something wrong, you can still respond out of love.

All too often, we point out the sin and faults in others while failing to see them in ourselves. We all have something in us that makes us less than perfect. She might be a prostitute, but you are a drunk. Although society has declared prostitution illegal and drinking legal, this doesn't make being a drunk less of a sin than being a prostitute. Both are wrong when you see them in a higher light.

Though few of us can achieve such a level, we can certainly try. We can act out of love instead of judgment or blame. How often do we measure people? We do it without even being aware of it. We size them up; assume that everyone in the trailer park is white trash, or that yuppies are better than those in the ghettos.

Revenge instantly shuts out love. Even a single thought of sticking it to someone will drive love away. Whatever justification you use, striking out at somebody, even in your thoughts, is wrong. Negativity and love can't stand side by side. One has to push the other out of the way. You can only channel your energy into one.

If you want love, then you have to put love out. You have to think love and be love. You have to shut out anything that stands against it and stop thinking those thoughts the minute they arise. The choice is yours; you can have any life that you want.

Heart meditation

In the last technique, I showed you how to open your heart chakra and how to ask your heart questions. Now I want you to pay attention to your heart, to listen to it without asking a question first or having any sort of an agenda.

I want you to once again breathe in the 2/4 rhythm and get into a meditative state. See your breath going to your heart, imagining it as pure white light. Now see a red sphere coming out of your heart. See it getting brighter and sparkling with divine energy.

Meditate on the sphere, clearing your mind of all thoughts and all distractions. Be open to anything that comes to you. You may have a thought, feel a feeling, or have an image pop into your head. Pay attention, your heart is talking to you.

Spiritual heart meditation

You need to anchor your love to the spirit world if you want it to be deep and meaningful. Spirituality doesn't mean attending church or following a certain dogma, but rather seeking a higher way than egocentric love and love that is centered around things. Many relationships run into trouble because they never rise above this level. The meditation below can help.

Get into a meditative state and see a sphere of pure white light at your heart. Now see a kite string going from this sphere up into the sky and into the spirit world. Hold this image in your mind for a moment and then let it fade. Now focus on the sphere and chant *shine,* seeing the sphere pulsate every time that you do so. Do this for at least five minutes a day and you will open up deeper, spiritual aspects of your love.

Carol H. had a good job, a new car, and a nice boyfriend, but she still wasn't happy. She wanted to marry, have a few kids, and to live the whole suburban dream, but she just wasn't happy about it. Any way that she turned seemed like drudgery.

Things seemed to be sent into hyperdrive when she got a promotion to another plant several hundred miles away. She would have more money, but Curt was having doubts about joining her. If she didn't go, she would have to find a new job. She feared that she wouldn't have enough money to make her car payments. It was at this time that I ran into her.

"So why are you so freaked out about making your car payments?" I asked.

"Because I have to, that's why." She ran her hand through her hair.

"You've always made your payments before," I said.

"That doesn't mean that I'm going to now. There's a lot of stuff coming down right now," she said.

"So what's coming down? I thought you were making a lot more money with this new move," I said.

"I don't know about this whole thing. If Curt doesn't come with me, then I don't think I'm going to take the job. Curt really doesn't want to go," she said.

"Can't you just stay at the job that you have now?" I asked.

Carol ran her hand through her hair once again, and then said, "I can't. If I don't take the promotion and move, then I'm out of a job. I'll probably never find another job that pays what this one does. I have to stay with this company."

Carol grew up in the country, but went to a suburban high school. The wealthier yuppie kids made fun of this simple girl from the country. Carol began to believe that she was inferior to others.

Carol made up for it by going to junior college and getting a degree in plastics. She went out and bought a brand new car, which she always kept sparkling clean.

"Does this go back to that high school stuff?" I asked her.

"It doesn't go back to anything. It's what's happening now." Carol ran her hand through her hair.

"Would it be so bad if you drove an older car? You'd still be with Curt," I said.

"I can't lose this job," she said.

"But you'll lose Curt. It's either the job or Curt," I said.

"I'll find a way to keep both. I have to," she said.

"Why do you care what those people said in high school? That was several years ago," I said.

"It has nothing to do with them," she said.

"Doesn't it?" I asked.

"If you're such a high and mighty guru or whatever you are, then why don't you tell me this big metaphysical answer?" She said.

"What those people in high school did to you was cruel. You chose to close your heart. Quit trying to be better than them and open your heart," I said.

Carol eyed me peculiarly and then looked away.

"I can teach you how to open your heart and to let go of what those people did to you in high school," I suggested.

Carol once again eyed me in a funny way.

"Do you want to live the rest of your life with a closed heart *and* with what those people did to you?" I looked her in the eye.

Carol remained motionless for a moment and then looked at me. She then asked, "What do I have to do?"

"Why don't you sit down and get comfortable," I said.

Carol sat down in a chair but fidgeted somewhat.

"I want you to focus on your breathing. Breathe in deeply and try to make both your inhalation and exhalation the same length. As you breathe in, I want you to hold the image of the people who tormented you in your mind. If you can, recall a particularly painful scene," I instructed.

"This isn't funny. What are you doing?" She snapped.

"I was just getting to that. Here's how you release it. Every time you inhale, I want you to say in your private speech *release this*. As you're doing this, I want you to visualize a sphere

111

of red light over your heart. As you continue to inhale, see the sphere getting brighter. See it get a little brighter each time you draw a breath," I instructed.

Carol gazed straight ahead, focusing on what she was doing. She kept going for another ten minutes. She then looked at me and said, "I couldn't visualize it any more. That's all I could do."

"That's fine. Do that every day and you will begin to see things turn around in no time at all," I said.

Carol left Curt and took the promotion. She made progress little by little, though was dealing with the issue surrounding her closed heart.

THE ARCHETYPE OF THE SOUL MATE

The best way to send your soul mate running to you is to send your soul mate your love. But there is a way to concentrate that love, a way to supercharge it so that it can't fail but to return to you in the form of your soul mate. Most people stumble onto their soul mate by accident while some people never meet their soul mate. Many mysteries surround this process, but it doesn't need to be this way.

Let's begin with your thoughts. Your thoughts affect much more than you believe, they shape the very reality that you live in. Every thought that you think affects the people around you, even those who are thousands of miles away. They will feel what you think, even if it's only on an unconscious level. Guard your thoughts as though you were speaking them aloud.

When you're pissed off or in a hurry, no one says anything to you. Some people may even gaze at you out of fear. But when you're happy and in a good mood, those same people will say *Hello* or *Good Morning* to you. So what's going on here? These people can't read your mind, but they are picking up on what you're thinking, albeit on an unconscious level.

In the same way, you can either attract or repel your soul mate. If you think angry thoughts regarding your soul mate, then your soul mate will think that you're angry at him. You can attract your soul mate in the same way, by thinking loving thoughts.

You can focus these loving thoughts and send them directly to your soul mate. Hold the image of yourself smiling in your thinking mind. Take a moment to let it build and then add some joy behind it. Now tell your soul mate, without visualizing anyone in particular, that you love her.

Your intentions can also either attract or repel your soul mate. Even if you lie in your thinking, others will unconsciously pick up on your intentions. You can get by with lying for a while, but your true nature will come shining through in the long run. People who are manipulative are very good at what they do, often spending their entire lifetime honing their skills. They will manipulate someone and then shower love on them. In this way, the manipulative act doesn't appear so mean. But they can't hide their intentions forever. Their true nature will come shining through, even if it takes the poor victim years to realize it.

Harvest the wind

You can use the wind to attract your soul mate. You must keep in mind that the wind, like all forces of nature, is spiritual. You need to respect this and not dismiss it too lightly. A breezy morning is the best to work in, but there shouldn't be a storm on the way because it will add negative energy behind your love, which could bring your anti-soul mate to you.

Find someplace where the breeze is blowing at a steady pace. Take a moment to stand there and let the wind blow against you. Stop to see that it is spiritual, this it was created by God, and that it is doing the work of God. As you experience it, smile and become joyful. Let this feeling build inside of you, and do your best to shut everything else out.

Look out into the wind, noticing that it is all around you. The wind goes on forever, having no beginning and no end. Though one gust may stop and another one start, you can't determine where the wind came from or where it's going. Know that somewhere out there your soul mate is feeling the same breeze blowing against her. Know that you are connected to your soul mate by that wind.

See a sphere of pure white light at your crown chakra and take a few moments to see it pulsate. Now, within the joy that you have built up, add your love to that emotion. Tell your soul mate that you love them, seeing your words being carried off by the wind. Know that your soul mate, who is somewhere inside that same wind, will get your message along with your emotions and intentions. Continue doing this for several minutes and continue to see the sphere of pure white light at your crown chakra pulsate.

Now, continue to be joyful and to have only loving thoughts in your mind. Tell your soul mate to step into your life, once again seeing the words roll out with the wind. Do this for several minutes and try to time your words with the breeze. This will send your soul mate running to you, and you'll be surprised at the way it happens.

Peggy G. was an attractive nurse with an active social life, but she just couldn't find her soul mate. She tried several dating services and took to going out every night, but nothing she did seemed to lead her in the right direction. It was during one trip to an Irish pub that she ran into me.

"Is there a way to find a guy who will stay with me longer than one night?" She asked.

"Do you want a guy to stay with you longer than one night?" I asked.

"Don't cop a Zen attitude on me," she said.

"Do you really want it unconsciously? Deep in your heart?" I asked her.

"Don't get heavy with me. I'm not really in the mood for any Zen New Age stuff," she said.

"I'm not getting heavy just to do it. I'm trying to help you," I said.

"So how will this heavy stuff get me a man?" She asked.

"By clearing away all the stuff that stands between you and what you want. Just look at your thoughts that consider it heavy stuff. Stop thinking that it is something that is opposed to you or something outside of you," I said.

"So what do I have to do?" She asked.

"The first thing you have to do is change your thinking. Quit thinking that it's separate from you, that it's 'out there' somewhere. This kind of thinking only serves to push your soul mate away," I said.

"So all I have to do is think about my soul mate coming to me and my soul mate will come to me?" She asked.

"For starters, but in your case I think you're going to have to be regressed," I said.

She sighed, and then said, "So let's get on with this heavy duty Zen stuff."

I led her out of that noisy pub and brought her back to her place. It didn't take me long to put her under after she had laid down on the couch. Though there were some noisy people outside, her apartment was quiet enough to allow a regression. I instructed her to go back to the lifetime where her trouble finding a man started. I asked her, "Have you returned to one of your past lives?"

"I think so," she said.

"Where are you? Describe it for me," I said.

"It's a big Indian camp, except it is more the size of a city. There are several thousand people there. There are tepees, animals, several fires for cooking, and hundreds of horses that are tied up," she said.

"What are you doing? Are you a man or a woman?" I asked.

"I'm a woman and I have a cleft upper lip. Part of my nose is also deformed," she said.

"Do you have a man? What are you doing?" I asked.

"I work with a group at one of the fires. I am cooking strips of Buffalo meat," she said.

"And do you have a boyfriend? How old are you?" I asked.

"I'm getting the impression that I'm twenty-three. I don't have a boyfriend. The men won't have anything to do with me, except to try and get sex from me. They think that because of my deformity, I'm easy," she said.

"And are you?" I asked.

"No, but I've slept with a couple of them. I don't want to get pregnant."

"Have you ever had a real boyfriend?" I asked.

"No," she choked back a few tears and then began to cry. She went on, "We had a big tribal celebration not long ago and I spent most of the time with the old women. The other young women of the tribe all have several men pursuing them, giving them food, drink, etc." She began to cry even harder. Tears streamed down her face.

"Okay, you know the cause. I want you to return to consciousness. You're coming back up now and on the count of 5 you will open your eyes. 1-2-3-4-5," I said.

When Peggy opened her eyes, she began to sob uncontrollably. She sat up and then lowered her head into her hands.

"It's okay. You understand the cause. We can now work on releasing it and moving on," I said.

"Oh God, I died alone and unloved," she sobbed.

"It's okay. It's not going to happen in this lifetime. Let go of the images. They're like an old TV program," I said.

"I can't get them out of my head," she said.

"Quit thinking about them. Think about something else. They'll fade in a minute. They're just like pictures from some old TV show," I said.

Peggy's life began to change not long after she realized the cause of her inability to find the love relationship she longed for. About a year and a half later, she was engaged to the man of her dreams.

Your actions, which are charged by your thoughts, also either attract or repel your soul mate. You can't walk around looking down your nose at people and expect love to come into your life. How you treat other people is how you treat yourself, for your actions will always come back to you, if not in this life, then in the next.

I know it's a tall order to act only in a loving way, but it's worth your while to try. The more love that you put out, the more love you will get back. You might feel justified in treating someone lower than you with a bully attitude and our society will stand behind your "right" to do so, but your bullying will return to you.

The way to handle it is to treat everyone that you come in contact with as a karmic test. How do you treat someone who's homeless and has a cardboard sign? Do you tell the "bum" to get a job? Do you give him a quarter? Do you walk by and pretend that he doesn't exist? You might have to take that test again.

Suppose that an aggressive panhandler blocks your path and insists that you give him a quarter. Suppose that he's dressed in fresh clothes, has showered, appears to have slept in a bed, and even to have a job. What do you do? You don't have to give him a quarter, but you can still act out of love.

If you want to respond more lovingly, it is a good idea to clean out your mental closets. Get rid of, and quit thinking, the negative and abusive thoughts that you have stored in your mind. The thought of "bum" or "get a job" that you think the moment someone asks you for a quarter. The ways that you curse or put down such a person in your thinking at the moment that they ask you for a quarter.

Send a valentine to your soul mate

There is one sure fire way to send your love to your soul mate that trumps everything else. Everything I've shown you up to this point has only been a warm up for this. This technique, which has never been revealed before, is the most powerful soul mate technique that has ever been invented.

Get the list of the qualities of what you want in your soul mate that you made in the first chapter. Take a few moments to read them over and calmly reflect on each one. You may want to add or subtract a few if you so desire.

See a sphere of pure white light at your crown chakra, taking a few moments to see it pulsate. Now breathe in the 2/4 rhythm and get into a meditative state. Take sufficient time to do this. Now take out your list of qualities. Meditate on the first one, saying it over and over again in your private speech. After a minute or so, mentally will the quality to come out of your third eye. See a red heart about 6 to 8 inches tall come out of your third eye and hover about three feet in front of you. See it glistening with energy and sparkling with red light. Now say to it in a loving manner:

Send my soul mate to me.

Now see the heart going away from you and disappearing out of sight. If you are inside, see it going through a wall or out a window. Know that it is going to your soul mate, but it is important not to visualize anyone in particular.

Do the same with the rest of your qualities, making sure to take your time. When you have finished, breathe in the 2/4 rhythm once again and get into a meditative state. Visualize your third eye closing and know that it is done. Your soul mate will come to you.

Just to supercharge it, everyday do the 2/4 breathing and get into a relaxed state. Send the heart out of your third eye chakra without putting a quality in it. Say to it:

Send my soul mate to me.

Send it on its way. Do this three times each day.

Karl B. was fast approaching forty and still hadn't found his soul mate. His problems were far deeper than that. Karl did time for domestic abuse twice, though he had done it several more times without being arrested. His father and uncle were both wife beaters and he nursed his mother back to health on many occasions.

Karl's most recent girlfriend left him after he got drunk one night and smacked her around. He ran into me several days later.

"I heard that you smacked Connie around. So what's going on?" I asked.

Karl blew out a sigh and then paced about for a few moments. He said while pacing, "I got drunk and I lost it."

"You seem to get drunk and lose it a lot," I pointed out.

"So what's it to ya?" He gazed down at his feet.

"You have to do something about it," I said.

"Like what? It runs in my family," he said.

"Have you tried counseling?" I asked.

"I've been to several shrinks. I've been to court shrinks, women's shrinks, family shrinks, and even special shrinks and none of them have done any good," he said.

"What about your father? Did he ever successfully break out of the cycle of beating your mother?" I asked.

Karl sighed heavily, and then said, "No, he died a wife beater. And it looks like I'm going to, too."

"There could be something from one of your past lives that is resulting in your violence. I think that you should explore it," I said.

Karl stopped fidgeting and looked me in the eye for the first time. He remained frozen for a moment, and then said, "Don't jive me with your New Age stuff."

"I'm not jiving you. I'm trying to help you," I said.

"It's not going to change anything. This is the way things are and there isn't a damn thing I can do about it," he said.

"Maybe there is something that you can do about it, if you'll give it a chance," I said.

"So what if I discover some long lost secret from one of my past lives, will it change anything?" He asked.

"Quite possibly," I said.

"But you won't guarantee me anything," he said.

"I can't guarantee you anything, but we usually find something significant. There's one sure way to find out," I said.

"Okay, but this better not take long," he said.

"It won't," I said.

I regressed Karl and instructed him to go back to the lifetime where his domestic violence began. Karl, though hypnotized, remained rather tense. I asked him, "So where are you?"

"I'm not sure," he replied.

"Ask your higher mind where you are," I instructed.

Karl remained quiet for a moment, and then said, "I'm in England during the Middle Ages. I'm working in a large brothel that isn't far from an Army camp. Business is brisk."

"Were you one of the women?" I asked.

"No, I was the man who kept everybody in line. I was a big mother and I took delight in pounding any man who got rough with one of the girls. I smacked the whores around whenever they mouthed off," he said.

"Did you smack them around often?" I asked.

"Everyday, but not the same ones," he said.

"And no one said anything to you about this?" I asked.

"The madam encourages me to do it. She often points out which one needs to be smacked around a little bit. She likes it when the women are quiet and kept in their place," he said.

"And how are the women responding?" I asked.

"They're terrified of me. Whenever they hear me walking toward them they straighten up and stop whatever they're doing," he said.

"I want to talk to your higher mind. I want to ask it if Karl's desire to control women, which now spans at least two lifetimes, is part of his violence toward women?" I asked.

"It's central," Karl said.

"Are there any other past lives that are influencing Karl's violence toward women?" I asked.

"Yes, there are a few, but there is one in particular that you should examine," Karl said.

"Go there now," I instructed.

"Okay, I'm starting to see it now," he said.

"So where are you?" I asked.

"I'm a monk in a Catholic monastery. The building is dim, damp, and drafty. The candles are spaced pretty wide in places," he said.

"So what are you doing?" I asked.

"I'm in charge of making bread. I'm working with a few other monks around a hearth," he said.

"What about women? Are there any women there?" I asked.

"There are a few nuns that live in another part of the building," he said.

"And did you have sex with any of them?" I asked.

"There's one nun who I've slept with," he said.

"And did you beat her?" I asked.

"The first time I approached her she didn't like my advances. She reminded me that we had taken vows. At that point, I didn't care. My desires were aroused and I wanted to have sex. I grabbed her and threw her down. She yelled, but the walls were too thick and there was no one else in that part of the building. I smacked her around and even punched her a couple of times. I ripped her clothes off and had my way with her," he said.

"Were you caught?" I asked.

"No. The nun never told. In fact she ran away a few nights later and was never heard from again," he said.

"Okay, I want you to return to consciousness. I'm going to count you down. When I get to one you will open your eyes and be wide-awake. 5-4-3-2-1," I said.

Karl opened his eyes and gazed about with a blank look on his face.

"Now you know that you beat women because you want to control them," I said.

"So what's the solution to all of this?" He looked at me with wide eyes.

"Give up your need to control," I said.

Karl returned to therapy and quickly made progress.

THE END OF THE JOURNEY

Once you have found your soul mate, you have come to the top the mountain and overcome much karma, some of which may stem from multiple incarnations. Though you may not be aware of it, you didn't make this journey alone. Others came in and out of your life and have helped you to advance spiritually, emotionally, and physically. This was no accident. You have known these people in several incarnations and they have come into your life at specific times to aid you. You have agreed to these meetings beforehand while in the spirit world preparing for this incarnation and your journey to your soul mate.

You need to see this as a karmic play that spans eternity and not as a random occurrence. These people connect you to the spirit world and make you more than a mere animal. Something larger is at play here, something much more than you just finding a mate to have a few children with. These people take you to levels that you wouldn't go to on your own, taking you beyond the realm of a mere dog. Animals have no spiritual reason for mating. They have no reason to marry and the female only needs the male to impregnate her.

You must start seeing things from the standpoint of eternity. You need to grasp the deeper meaning of that painful break-up. This is hard when you are charged with emotion, which consumes your entire thought life. By seeing it from the point of view of eternity, you will see it not as a single emotional event, but rather as a stepping stone on your continuing journey.

Here is a meditation that will allow you to see such events from the point of view of eternity. Get into a meditative state. See a sphere of pure white light at your crown chakra. Take a few moments to see it pulsate. Now see yourself out in the universe, visualizing a galaxy close to you. Look back at the Earth and see yourself in pain from the break-up. Hold this image for several minutes and you will see your break-up in proper perspective.

Each of the events that you go through are actually stepping stones on your eternal journey of advancement and unfolding. Society presents us with a false view of these things. This is reinforced by Hollywood, which turns out movie after movie about such things. The break-up is seen in terms of ego things, which have no spiritual aspect about it at all. The ego, which behaves like an infant that wants immediate gratification and everything to be its way and its way only, will make things even worse by clinging and blaming.

Our society is ego driven and egocentric with a full line of consumer products to satisfy its every whim and desire. The ego is a thumb sucking infant, one that is a spoiled brat, a brat that throws a tantrum if it doesn't get its way. We have instant soul mates in our society. Web sites, etc promise to match you up with the person of your dreams. Many people meet someone online and actually believe that they are in love with this person based upon emails and text messages only. You must set your sights much higher.

Many people fail to complete their journey to the end that is destined for them. They end up marrying the wrong person and thus advance little spiritually. Such marriages are like dogs who fornicate for offspring, each dog going its separate way after the sex act has been completed. The thumb sucking and infantile ego will never be satisfied, and the path to spiritual advancement that the soul mate brings the ego on, will be left behind in the dust. Relationships that are based on sex, looks, money, etc are such relationships.

Possessions are a spiritual poison that derails many from even starting their journey, let alone reaching the end of it. Value judgments are made based upon what someone owns, or doesn't own. Possessions are a cheap substitute for love in our society. Many workaholic parents hand their children everything, falsely believing that it is the same as love. The child ends up feeling empty and fails to seek anything higher than what is before its eyes.

You need to see things from a higher perspective, viewing them from the point of view of eternity. You need to see the journey that you are on, and the spiritual advancement that goes with it, in order to see the end of the journey. Most people have no idea where they are going in life, drifting from one lover to another, one job to another, one town to another, etc.

Here is a meditation that will allow you to see that the people who come into your life aren't merely a random occurrence. You will clearly come to see that there is a higher order to everything that has happened in your life. Once you realize this, it is hoped you will see possessions and relationships that are based on sex, etc for the delusions that they are.

Get into a meditative state. See a sphere of pure white light at your crown chakra and see it pulsate for a few minutes. See a beam of white light come from this pulsating chakra and shine onto yourself at a specific moment in your past. You will see a scene from your past and a person who has helped you grow spiritually in some way. To get further details as to just what that person did and how they helped you, you need to do a simple meditation. Get into a meditative state. See yourself standing in front of a mirror. See a sphere of pure white light at your crown chakra and see it pulsating. See the scene and person in your mind that you saw in the meditation above and you will see your answer in the mirror. You should do both of these meditations for critical points in your life and at different ages.

Once you have met your soul mate, a new journey unfolds. The end of the journey is really the beginning. "End" and "beginning" are two names and forms that describe the same thing. Let go of both of them and you will see the journey from the point of view of eternity, as it is meant to be seen. The family that you will have together is also for spiritual advancement. See it, and accept it, as an opportunity for growth.

If you have an autistic child, it is because that child will help you grow and provide you with an opportunity to balance your karma. Biology, genetics, etc are merely players—the *effect*—and not the *cause* of the problem. Don't look to medicine for solutions because to do so is to relegate the human race to the status of an animal. Seek a higher point of view and higher answers.

Your family will also provide you with an opportunity to teach your children and others and to share your gifts. Your children will teach you as well, often in ways that you don't expect. Your son's pot smoking may be a lesson for you to lighten up and to quit judging people who are different from yourself. Instead of yelling and trying to force your son to be exactly as you want him to be, stop and pay attention to the lesson that is being taught to you.

God within your unconscious, what Jung termed the Self, is always leading you to wholeness and advancement on your journey *if you will only listen to it.* Pay attention to your hunches and urges, especially those that happen more than once. The more you work with it, the more your deeper mind will open up to you, and the easier it will be to receive guidance from the Self.

Your dreams can also provide you with guidance on your journey, but you have to learn how to interpret the symbolism. Reading a book on Jungian dream interpretation can help you greatly. The Self will kick you in the head in order to get through to you, so pay attention to recurring dreams. The Self won't seem so strange once you learn to speak its language and come to trust it to aid you on your journey.

Advancement along this path is analogous to a hot air balloon taking off. The balloon isn't going to get off the ground if countless sand bags are tied to it. In order to go up, and go up fast, you need to cast off all of the sand bags. Many people want to go up, but they cling to sand bags full of garbage from their past that they refuse to let go. You need to cut these ropes physically, in your thinking, and emotionally. Then, and only then, will your balloon take flight.

As you advance along this path, new things will open up for you. These new things weren't available to you at the lower levels because you weren't spiritually advanced enough. Thus your soul mate will only come to you when you are spiritually ready. Most people describe it as some sort of magic door that opens. Feelings that you have known this person from your past, giddy feelings, and feelings of being connected to the spirit world are all quite common when a soul mate comes into the picture.

Meeting your soul mate at a point where you aren't spiritually advanced enough to do so is like meeting a stranger in the street. It isn't going to help you any. Your soul mate won't take you to new levels or help you complete the karmic mission (which your soul mate has incarnated at this time to help you with), if you aren't ready. If you are to meet your soul mate on a cloud at five hundred feet and your balloon is still weighted down with sand bags, then there is no way for you to advance in order to meet him/her.

As I have said, the end of your journey is the beginning of a new and higher journey. At higher levels of spiritual advancement, you will graduate to new things, things that weren't possible before. As we have seen throughout this book, you will unfold in ways that you have never expected. You will do things that you dreaded in the past. Many men who had no desire to have children, and some who even hated the idea, have gone on to have several children with their soul mate.

Once you reach the end of your journey, you will let go of some of the sand bags of old karma that you have been carrying around, some for many incarnations, and open up new doors to spiritual advancement. What you do here will shape not only this incarnation, but future incarnations to come. All of this is only possible if you will cast off those sand bags and ascent to new spiritual heights. Will you climb all the way to the end of your journey?

About the Author

Tom Arbino (born Thomas Anthony Arbino on November 16, 1958 in Cincinnati, Ohio) is an American novelist, playwright, poet, and the founder of Crown Chakra Zen. Tom writes novels and short stories in various genres, which deal with things outside of the mainstream. Tom's novel *Lots Rigged by a Phantom* is set in the1800s and deals with the horrors of an insane captain, a wicked sea monster, and an arrogant ghost. Tom's short story collection, *The Alchemist's Pocket Watch* is a collection of his horror stories and features a novella. Tom's plays are controversial and not afraid to tackle the heated issues of the day. These plays shed light on things that need to be dealt with and not repressed. Such plays as *Talk Show, Crisis Point, Cafe Marseille, Monkey Bars, The Adventures of Bill and Hillary and The Hands of the Father* bear this out. Tom listens to Old Time Radio and his favorites are: X minus 1, Dimension X, and Jack Benny. Tom says that these shows develop his imagination, creativity, and hone his playwriting skills. (It is best to listen to these shows with your eyes closed since we are so visually oriented these days.) Tom has written a radio play entitled *The Last Train to Tombstone.* Tom has published a book of poetry entitled *Anarchy* that contains Beat and anarchy poetry that is reminiscent of the Beat Poetry of the 1960s such as Jack Kerouac, Neal Cassady and Allen Ginsberg. This book also contains sections of Zen poetry and love poetry. Tom is the Arts and Entertainment reporter for the Cincinnati Edition of EXAMINER.COM

Tom grew up in a cracker box house neighborhood on the east sided of Cincinnati. Tom's imagination was sparked early in life by TV shows Lost in Space, Mission impossible, The Invaders,

Sea hunt, Batman, Marine Boy, and Flipper. These shows provided him an escape from his abusive mother and an older girl next door who molested him beginning at the age of 10.

Tom holds an AAS in Civil Engineering Technology from Cincinnati Technical College and a BA in psychology from the University of Cincinnati. Tom completed 33 hours toward s a master's degree in mental health counseling. Tom studied Jungian Psychology at Mt. St. Mary's Seminary. Tom works as a web site designer. He tried his hand at game making and produced one Atari style game called Alley Kong.

Tom has read much of Carl Jung's works and has analyzed over 20,000 dreams using his training in Jungian Psychology. Using Jungian Psychology, Tom has accessed the Self, God within the unconscious. Tom has access the Self, analyzed its archetypes, and brought it up into consciousness with the aid of Zen meditation techniques.

Tom's study of Zen was undertaken for spiritual development and his frustration with outwardly oriented mainstream churches that offer little beyond Dogma. The Zen that Tom developed, Crown Chakra Zen, is distinct from Zazen based Zen and is the First American school of Zen. Tom is not a Buddhist.

Other Books Published
by
Ozark Mountain Publishing, Inc.

Continue for more books by Ozark Mountain Publishing, Inc.

For more information about any of the above titles, soon to be released titles, or other items in our catalog, write or visit our website:

OZARK
MOUNTAIN
PUBLISHING

PO Box 754
Huntsville, AR 72740
www.ozarkmt.com
1-800-935-0045/479-738-2348
Wholesale Inquiries Welcome